the **dog** directory

P
i

hamlyn | all colour
the **dog** directory

Facts, figures and profiles of over 100 breeds

Chas Newkey-Burden

hamlyn

Thanks to Chris Morris and Barnaby

An Hachette UK Company
www.hachette.co.uk

First published in Great Britain in 2009 by
Hamlyn, a division of Octopus Publishing Group Ltd
2-4 Heron Quays, London E14 4JP
www.octopusbooks.co.uk

Copyright © Octopus Publishing Group Ltd 2009

ISBN 978-0-600-61829-4

A CIP catalogue record for this book is available from
the British Library

Printed and bound in China

10 9 8 7 6 5 4 3 2 1

The advice in this book is provided as general
information only. It is not necessarily specific to
any individual case and is not a substitute for the
guidance and advice provided by a licensed
veterinary practitioner consulted in any particular
situation. Octopus Publishing Group accepts no
liability or responsibility for any consequences
resulting from the use of or reliance upon the
information contained herein.

No dogs or puppies were harmed in the making
of this book.

DogsTrust

Dogs Trust is the UK's largest dog welfare charity
and campaigns on dog welfare issues to ensure
a safe and happy future for all dogs. The charity
has a network of 17 centres across the UK and
cares for over 16,000 stray and abandoned dogs
each year. The charity is well known for its
slogan 'A Dog Is For Life, Not Just For Christmas'
and is working towards the day when all dogs
can enjoy a happy life, free from the threat of
unnecessary destruction.

If you are interested in rehoming a dog
you can visit the Dogs Trust website at
www.dogstrust.org.uk and click on Rehoming,
or call **020 7837 0006** to find your nearest centre.

Registered charity numbers 227523 and SC037843

Contents

Introduction

Dogs have been our close companions for thousands of years. They have guarded, guided, transported, entertained and even fed us, and over time we have bred and refined them to create breeds to fulfil particular roles and to exhibit specific, desirable characteristics.

This guide to all the best-loved breeds will help you understand the canine world. The first section gives an overview of how and why different dog breeds were developed, including an outline of the main categories of dog.

The second section features profiles of more than 100 dog breeds, each blending practical information with quirkier details. You can discover whether Bulldogs are good with children, why Shar Peis frown and which dog was bred to be eaten. Finally, there is a guide to which dogs are best for first-time owners, sedentary owners, city-dwellers, families, and so on.

Whether you are considering buying a dog or whether you simply want to understand more about the one you already own or would just like to know a little more about these endearing and faithful animals, this is the book for you.

The history of dog breeds

Most experts agree that the dogs we know today are descended from the Eurasian wolf. Studies of the physiology of the earliest domesticated dogs reveal creatures that had the head shape and stature of young wolves, and these early dogs were apparently bred to be slightly tamer versions of the wolf. However, this was just the beginning of a remarkable story.

Humans first intervened in the breeding of dogs around 12,000 years ago, when it was found that the animals could be bred specifically for everything from hunting to warfare and from friendship to food. In the process the domestic dog has become the most varied species of animal, and today there is far greater diversity within the species than there is in any other species of domestic animal, including the cat.

The oldest recorded breeds of dog include the Pharaoh Hound, depictions of which have been found in the tombs of ancient Egyptian

pharaohs, and the Canaan Hound, which guarded flocks and camps in the Middle East in pre-biblical times. The descendants of the Pharaoh Hound are the sighthounds, among the earliest of which were the Sloughi and Saluki, which were originally bred to hunt gazelles in the Arabian deserts. Then came the Afghan Hound, which as well as hunting was also used to guard homes in Afghanistan. Just as dogs were given defensive roles, so too were they given offensive ones, and it was in ancient Rome that Molossians, the forebears of the Mastiff breed, were used as attack dogs in battle.

In colder areas, such as Alaska, Russia and the Arctic regions, dogs were bred for different purposes. The Alaskan Malamute pulled sleds across the snow, while in Finland the Karelian Bear Dog was used for hunting. Dogs bred to guard livestock had to be large and fearless so that they would stand up to predators such as bears, lions, wolves and even fellow dogs. Meanwhile, in Tibet the Pug was bred to guard temples — and a very good job they did. In nearby China and Korea, dogs were bred to be eaten.

Some breeds were developed for quite specific roles. The Lundehund, for example, was bred to capture puffins from their nests in northern Norway, the breed's flexibility and extra toe on each forepaw making it ideal for reaching into rocks and crevices. The Coonhound, on the other hand, was developed for tracking and treeing raccoons and other forest quarry. The Duck Tolling Retriever was bred with a white tip on its tail to arouse the curiosity of waterfowl, which were then shot by the hunter.

Just as dogs were being bred to work on behalf of humans, they were increasingly refined for their appearance and temperament. The rulers of China, India and Europe began to breed dogs almost as fashion accessories, and it was not long before aristocratic women wanted small, affectionate dogs that could be companions and lap dogs. Not that attractive dogs were necessarily without other roles. The Dalmatian's spotted coat is fashionable, but one of the dog's original tasks was to run alongside carriages, clearing the road for ease of passage.

This is a story without end as dogs continue to be bred for new purposes. The Labradoodle, for instance, combines the trainability of the Labrador Retriever with the low-shedding coat of the Poodle, thereby creating a guide dog suitable for blind and partially-sighted people with allergies to fur. In the same way, the Cockerpoo has the outgoing and affectionate nature of the Cocker Spaniel with the low-shedding trait of the Poodle.

Among all this talk of breeds, let us not forget mongrels. The mongrel or mixed-breed dog is often healthier than the pure-breed equivalents because the genes that cause health problems are watered down within a larger gene pool. These dogs often live much longer than pure breeds, and for this reason they make ideal family pets.

Dog breeds

Dogs are divided into seven main groups – Gundogs, Hounds,
Pastoral Dogs, Terriers, Toy Dogs, Utility Dogs and Working Dogs –
each of which has specific traits and characteristics.

Gundogs

These dogs were bred to help with shooting
and hunting. The setting breeds were
charged with the task of locating the game,
spaniels were employed to move the game
and other spaniels would 'flush' the game so
that hunters could shoot it. The retrievers
would do just what their names suggest.

Because they have worked so closely and
successfully with humans, these are normally
obedient and friendly dogs. Gundogs are
generally active, intelligent
and reliable, and few
of them are noisy.

They enjoy life with an active family and are
generally good with children.

The sizes of dogs in this group range from
the strapping Labrador Retriever to the small
Cocker Spaniel. There is also little uniformity
in coat type, with the curly-coated Irish Water
Spaniel, the straight-haired Irish Setter and
the short-coated Pointer providing plenty of
contrast and differing grooming demands.

Hounds

One of the oldest groups of dogs, the Hounds
were bred to help chase and catch quarry.
Some of these breeds, therefore, should not
be included in households with small pets,
particularly pets that are introduced to the
home after the dog.

Although these active and intelligent dogs are usually sociable and amiable, they are not unhappy with owners who are a little detached. Because their original role required a large degree of independence, many of the breeds in the group exhibit a streak of autonomy and even disobedience.

This is a wonderfully diverse group, including not only the sleek sighthounds, such as Greyhounds and Borzois, and the more sturdily built scenthounds, such as Basset Hounds and Beagles, but also the tiny Dachshunds.

Pastoral Dogs

This relatively new group includes some breeds that used to be in the working category. These dogs were bred to work closely with humans,

generally herding or protecting livestock, and they are, therefore, usually energetic, hardworking dogs, which tend to form close bonds with their owners.

A common characteristic is the dogs' tendency to obey their owners' commands but also to use their own judgement. They are in the main, however, biddable dogs, both affectionate and easily trained.

There are many sizes, colours and coat types in this group, the best known of which are the Collies, Welsh Corgis and German Shepherd Dogs.

Terriers

Terriers were first bred to catch and kill animals, either as nascent pest-controllers or for sport. This means that they are often predatory and energetic, and some like digging. They can make good watchdogs.

Busy and exuberant, these dogs can be aggressive towards other pets, both canine and non-canine, and some of them can be

quite stubborn. However, their outgoing and friendly nature makes them popular.

This group shows the least variation among breeds, most Terriers being either in the short-legged or long-legged breeds. Bull Terriers are feisty dogs, while Cesky Terriers and Scottish Terriers are more placid.

Toy Dogs

These dogs were originally bred to be companions, and that continues to be their role. Because their working tendencies have been largely bred out of them, they are generally placid and friendly. However, the selective breeding that made them small also made many of them susceptible to health problems.

Dogs in this group are generally ideal for the first-time owner. They are usually cooperative and even-tempered and tend to be eager to please. However, although they

are often small in size, they have plenty of personality and are full of spirit.

This group contains a wide range of breeds, from the energetic, stubborn and noisy Yorkshire Terrier to the calm and collected Pekingese, and from the sleek Italian Greyhound to the bulkier Bolognese.

Utility Dogs

This particularly diverse group includes dogs that were originally developed to carry out a particular task but that in more recent times have been bred solely for companionship. The breeds range from distinctive and eccentric dogs, such as the Chow Chow and Schnauzer, to family favourites like the Dalmatian and the Poodle. In fact, the dogs in this group are those that cannot be included elsewhere, and it is, therefore, best to judge each breed on its individual merits.

Working Dogs

Dogs in this group are keen on activity and require stimulation. Over the years their courage and sturdy build have been used by humans in all manner of ways, including pulling carts and for rescue and protection. They are, therefore, usually intelligent, trainable and robust.

These tend to be fiercely loyal dogs, which do best when they are with owners who not only have previous experience of handling dogs but who are also mentally and physically strong and capable of standing up to their pets. Some of these dogs do not mix well with small children or other pets.

The group ranges from the huge Mastiff and Bernese Mountain Dog to the comparatively small Boxer, Dobermann and Pinschers. Courageous and alert, Working Dogs are formidable in every way.

The pawprints

 Each profile contains a summary of the breed's main characteristics. In addition to its size and weight, the breed's need for exercise, suitability as a family pet and maintenance requirements are marked out of five. Five pawprints indicate, for example, that a breed needs plenty of exercise, while two pawprints show that the breed would be suitable for a less energetic owner.

English Setter

Exuberant yet easy-going

Size 61–69 cm (24–27 in)
Weight 25–30 kg (55–66 lb)
Exercise needs 🐾 🐾 🐾 🐾 🐾
Family pet? 🐾 🐾 🐾 🐾
Maintenance 🐾 🐾 🐾 🐾

Bred for: Flushing and retrieving birds
An English Setter is effervescent, patient and vocal

English Setters have been blessed with generous helpings of elegance and grace, but owners should watch out for a wild, rather dictatorial streak that is common in the breed. However, a dog's wilful side can be minimized with correct training and handling, leaving the owner with a gentle, endearing and good natured pet.

Although they are challenging to train, English Setters are kindly dogs, which want to please their owners. Their ideal home environment is with an active family in a neighbourhood with plenty of areas for off-lead walks. Outgoing and vocal, they make excellent watchdogs.

The breed's chief attraction lies in its silky, feathery coat, but this does have the drawback of attracting mud and twigs during walks, which must be removed. The dogs need regular brushing and shampooing, which can be time-consuming affairs.

When they are indoors English Setters are tranquil and quiet, but when they are out on a walk they become lively and energetic. The dogs were originally bred to run throughout the day, so they are bursting with energy and need lengthy periods of exercise on a regular basis. The breathtaking sight of your English Setter in full flight will more than reward your efforts.

Gordon Setter

Devoted and outgoing

Size 62–66 cm (24½–26 in)
Weight 25.5–29.5 kg (55–65 lb)
Exercise needs 🐾 🐾 🐾 🐾 🐾
Family pet? 🐾 🐾 🐾 🐾
Maintenance 🐾 🐾 🐾

Bred for: Flushing birds
A Gordon Setter is exuberant, active and assured

It is sometimes said that dogs become like their owners, but here it's more a case of the reverse needing to be true. Animated and energetic, Gordon Setters demand the same qualities in their owners, and regular, long walks and runs are essential.

The heaviest of the setters, Gordon Setters have wavy black and tan coats with heavy feathering, which need daily attention. Despite having a stubborn streak, they are easy dogs to train, although their powerful build can make them problematic in households with small children.

Affectionate and calm by nature, these are friendly, loyal dogs. They are also fun and full of stamina, and among the games they enjoy during exercise are swimming and ball games. However, when they are denied adequate opportunities for activity, they will try to escape.

These are truly protective dogs, but on occasion they can be jealous. Handled correctly and with early training, however, they are steadfast and reliable companions, which will delight a suitable owner and make a sociable family pet.

Irish Red and White Setter
Obedient and sensitive

Size 58–69 cm (23–27 in)
Weight 27–32 kg (60–70 lb)
Exercise needs 🐾 🐾 🐾 🐾
Family pet? 🐾 🐾 🐾 🐾
Maintenance 🐾 🐾 🐾

Bred for: Flushing and retrieving game
An Irish Red and White Setter is kind, agreeable and frolicsome

Heedful and full of life, Irish Red and White Setters are great family dogs. They are affectionate towards their owners and generally get along well with children, other pets and unfamiliar dogs. Their exuberance often proves to be contagious.

That said, however, they are challenging dogs to control and are one of the trickier breeds of Gundog to train. They mean well, though, so your persistence will be quickly rewarded. The Irish Red and White Setter tends to mature slowly, so their owners will need plenty of patience, too.

Potential owners must be aware that these dogs need plenty of exercise. They love regular runs outdoors, when their feathery coats attract plenty of dirt. If they are denied sufficient exercise, they will become hyperactive and might try to escape.

Despite their active nature, these dogs are only moderate eaters, and even at their most exuberant their good nature is to the fore. They are also highly intelligent and will bring much joy to a suitable owner. This is a breed associated with the countryside and it will be normally at its happiest there.

Irish Setter

Affectionate and exuberant

Size 64–69 cm (25–27 in)
Weight 27–32 kg (60–70 lb)
Exercise needs 🐾 🐾 🐾 🐾
Family pet? 🐾 🐾 🐾 🐾
Maintenance 🐾 🐾 🐾

Bred for: Flushing game
An Irish Setter is lively, friendly and fun

A boisterous bundle of happy-go-lucky energy, the Irish Setter lives life with joy, and as long as you are able to devote sufficient time and expend sufficient energy to keep up with their needs, this breed could be a fantastic addition to your home.

Irish Setters exhibit plenty of affection towards their owners, but you should bear in mind that affection and obedience are quite different things. These are wilful dogs with excellent memories, so any bad habits they pick up during their early years will be difficult to train out of them later.

The richly coloured, deep chestnut coats give the dogs a distinctly glamorous air, but keeping the coats beautiful involves regular cleaning and brushing to achieve a smooth, mat-free sheen, not to mention periodic clipping of the feathered fur.

Good natured and easy-going, Irish Setters will be at their happiest living in large homes with active families, where they have access to areas where they can run and romp at will. The dogs are good with children, although they might be too exuberant for the smallest members of a family.

Pointer

Alert and active

Size 61–69 cm (24–27 in)
Weight 20–30 kg (44–66 lb)
Exercise needs 🐾 🐾 🐾 🐾
Family pet? 🐾 🐾 🐾
Maintenance 🐾 🐾

Bred for: Flushing and pointing to game
A Pointer is bright, intelligent and observant

Pointers are extremely sharp-minded dogs with colossal reserves of energy and stamina. They therefore need regular long walks and plenty of mental stimulation. The responsibility for the first lies with their owners, of course, but these dogs will find plenty of the latter for themselves as they follow a scent. They have acute hearing as well as a keen sense of smell, and are usually intelligent, bright dogs.

Effortlessly athletic, Pointers maintain their impressive dignity even when they are galloping at full speed. Deny them plentiful stimulation, however, and they will become bored and destructive surprisingly quickly.

The closely related German Shorthaired Pointers and German Wirehaired Pointers are smaller and are somewhat more easy-going, particularly the Shorthaired breed. Both share the Pointer's need for exercise.

Their nose-to-the-ground posture on walks is distinctive and charming. The coats are easy to maintain, and Pointers usually live to a ripe old age. That long life is best spent with an active, sociable family living in a spacious home.

Chesapeake Bay Retriever
Loyal and alert

Size 55–66 cm (21–26 in)
Weight 32–33 kg (70–80 lb)
Exercise needs 🐾 🐾 🐾 🐾
Family pet? 🐾 🐾 🐾
Maintenance 🐾 🐾 🐾

Bred for: Retrieving waterfowl
A Chesapeake Bay Retriever is independent, determined and bold

Do you enjoy going for long walks, even on cold or wet days? If you do, a Chesapeake Bay Retriever could be just the dog for you. The breed's coat helps to insulate them against adverse weather, which will make no difference at all to their desire for exercise. They will romp across green fields and mud, and their coats will collect plenty of dirt along the way.

One of the bravest of retrievers, Chesapeake Bay Retrievers tend to be reserved with strangers, as is the related Curly Coated Retriever. This latter dog is larger and has the distinctive curly coat from which its name is derived. Both breeds love opportunities to swim.

The strongly independent streak that is found running through both breeds means that they can be a handful to train, and their ideal owners will have an abundance of confidence so that they can deal with these hardy dogs correctly.

Territorial problems can sometimes arise between Chesapeake Bay Retrievers and other pets, but these remain popular and gratifying members of an active household.

Golden Retriever

Obedient and determined

Size 51–61 cm (20–24 in)
Weight 27–36 kg (60–80 lb)
Exercise needs 🐾 🐾 🐾 🐾
Family pet? 🐾 🐾 🐾 🐾 🐾
Maintenance 🐾 🐾

Bred for: Retrieving game
A Golden Retriever is bright, cheerful and kindly

The enormous popularity of Golden Retrievers is simple to understand: they are extremely cheerful, good-natured and intelligent dogs. Apparently big fans of the human race, they are enthusiastic and responsive towards their owners.

Golden Retrievers are not just responsive; they are also highly obedient, making them one of the easiest of dogs to train. They must, however, be taught early not to pull on the lead. They have forgiving natures and are also patient and gentle, making them very well-suited companions for children and easy-going with other animals.

They are exuberant and powerful dogs, so they need regular exercise, including long walks and plenty of games, with lots of retrieval-based play, and they also enjoy swimming. They do have a tendency to chew objects, which is best addressed by providing them with plenty of toys they can carry in their mouths.

With their welcoming bark and gently demonstrative nature, Golden Retrievers are generous with their affections. They combine relaxed good manners in the home with athleticism and playfulness out of doors. It's a winning formula.

Labrador Retriever

Exuberant and acquiescent

Size 55–57 cm (21½–22½ in)
Weight 25–34 kg (55–75 lb)
Exercise needs 🐾 🐾 🐾 🐾
Family pet? 🐾 🐾 🐾 🐾 🐾
Maintenance 🐾 🐾 🐾

Bred for: Retrieving game and, originally, assisting fishermen with their nets
A Labrador Retriever is versatile, water-loving and popular

Usually known simply as Labradors, these are ideal dogs for the first-time owner. They are affectionate, patient and playful. Not only are they brilliant with children, they are also loyal and intelligent, so it should come as no surprise that these dogs are one of the most popular breeds across the world.

Labrador Retrievers are high-spirited and energetic, and they require regular exercise, including long walks. They adore playing with the family and are keen swimmers. Their waterproof, drip-dry coats are reasonably low maintenance when it comes to grooming.

Although they are easily trained, these dogs are strong and must be taught at an early age not to pull on the leash. They have a huge, demanding appetite for food, so their owners must control their intake of food to avoid obesity. Easily bored if left alone for long periods, they can become destructive.

Steadfast and loving, Labrador Retrievers are superb family pets, and anyone looking for a devoted, enthusiastic companion with a lust for life would not go far wrong with this breed, which come with yellow, black or chocolate coats.

Yellow coat

Chocolate coat

Black coat

American Cocker Spaniel

Keen and gentle

Size 34–39 cm (13½–15½ in)
Weight 11–13 kg (24–28 lb)
Exercise needs 🐾 🐾 🐾 🐾
Family pet? 🐾 🐾 🐾
Maintenance 🐾 🐾 🐾

Bred for: Retrieving small game
An American Cocker Spaniel is wilful, amiable and cheerful

If you are the sort of person who is happy to put in plenty of time walking, grooming and playing with a dog, the cheerful American Cocker Spaniel might be for you. Certainly, one look into the adorable brown eyes would tempt many.

A possible drawback, however, is the requirement for regular, careful grooming. The breed's long coat is undoubtedly attractive, but it must have meticulous care to stay that way, requiring to be cleaned after most walks as well as needing a daily brush and regular cuts.

Notably gentle dogs, American Cocker Spaniels are easily trained. However, they can be intimidated by too strong a hand, and they have been to known to become needy if their independent side is not encouraged.

Although they appreciate good country walks, these small dogs can live happily in the city, and they do not require a particularly large home. Willing to please, they certainly succeed in their aim. True, they can also be unresponsive at times but this is not born out of any malice and will be countered by sensible training.

Parti-colour
coat

Tricolour
coat

English Cocker Spaniel
Wilful and affectionate

Size 38–41 cm (15–16 in)
Weight 14–14 kg (28–32 lb)
Exercise needs 🐾 🐾 🐾 🐾
Family pet? 🐾 🐾 🐾 🐾
Maintenance 🐾 🐾 🐾 🐾

Bred for: Retrieving small game
An English Cocker Spaniel is busy, bouncy and curious

These compact little dogs are happy and enthusiastic, and a typical walk with one will see the dog busily searching around among the vegetation following its natural instincts. The breed in general requires plenty of such walks, because English Cocker Spaniels need even more exercise than their American equivalents. They are also keen swimmers.

Compared to the sweet playfulness exhibited by the puppies, adult English Cocker Spaniels tend to have stubborn, rather wilful characters. However, as long as they are handled with the appropriate level of respect, they make willing and fast learners and respond well to gentle but firm training.

The beautiful, feathery coat will need daily attention, and the long hair on their characteristic floppy ears needs especial care because it can tangle easily. These dogs also benefit from regular trimming or clipping from a professional.

If the breed had a motto, it would be to live life to the full. It's a noble ambition and one that should be shared by any owner.

English Springer Spaniel
Resilient and sociable

Size 46–48 cm (18–19 in)
Weight 16–20 kg (35–45 lb)
Exercise needs 🐾 🐾 🐾 🐾
Family pet? 🐾 🐾 🐾 🐾
Maintenance 🐾 🐾 🐾 🐾

Bred for: Flushing, springing and retrieving game
An English Springer Spaniel is nimble, friendly and tireless

English Springer Spaniels are cheerful, rather impish dogs, and their exuberance and zest for life itself are infectious. Admittedly, their high spirits can on occasion verge on boisterousness, but these dogs are keen to please and respond well to correct handling.

The gregariousness of the breed stretches to humans, fellow dogs and other pets, and as long as they are being mentally and physically engaged, their charming, tail-wagging ways will be to the fore. They take well to retrieval games.

The medium-length coat needs daily attention, and those enchanting long ears must also be cared for to avoid tangles and other problems. They are not huge eaters, despite their tireless approach to life.

Training must be done early and with a reasonably firm hand. A successful outcome will see these dogs happy to romp while they are out of doors and be reasonably calm and obedient when they are in the home.

The characteristic feathering needs grooming and occasional trimming.

Weimaraner

Caring and obedient

Size 56–69 cm (22–27 in)
Weight 32–39 kg (70½–86 lb)
Exercise needs 🐾 🐾 🐾 🐾 🐾
Family pet? 🐾 🐾 🐾 🐾
Maintenance 🐾 🐾

Bred for: Tracking, hunting, pointing and retrieving
A Weimaraner is exuberant, active and athletic

Weimaraners are sleek and stylish, and when they are in motion they carry themselves with a particularly athletic grace. Their striking eyes merely add to their beauty. But what of their character? Weimaraners are brimful of passion and exuberance. They are friendly, alert and gentle dogs, and they also obey orders and are extremely protective of their owner.

Wonderfully good-natured, these dogs will get along with most people. However, families with very young children or small pets should hesitate before they add a Weimaraner to their household because they can inadvertently trample small people and animals underfoot.

Keen to learn and please, they are easy dogs to train. Their thin coats are as low maintenance as they come, although the dogs can feel the cold in the winter months.

Weimaraners are dogs for active owners. They need plenty of exercise, and an ideal day would involve abundant, playful exercise followed by a relaxing cuddle with their owner. This is a classy-looking dog with bountiful good points.

Kooikerhondje
Industrious and energetic

Size 35–40 cm (14–16 in)
Weight 9–11 kg (20–24 lb)
Exercise needs 🐾 🐾 🐾 🐾
Family pet? 🐾 🐾 🐾 🐾
Maintenance 🐾 🐾 🐾

Bred for: Hunting ducks in the Netherlands
A Kooikerhondje is loyal, busy but wary of strangers

Kooikerhondjes (or Kooiker Hound) are delightfully mixed bags. They are steadfast yet sensitive; generous yet territorial. Their delightful expression says it all, exuding as it does both agility and calm.

The white and orange-red coats will attract dirt, despite being waterproof, while the dogs are on walks, and this will come back into the home with them. That aside, they are simple dogs to groom, and an occasional brushing to remove dead hair will usually suffice.

Kooikerhondjes do need to be kept active. They are agile dogs and need regular exercise, and they will quickly become bored if they are not given things to occupy their minds. Although this makes them fairly demanding, they take so well to fun of any kind that their owners will feel recompensed for their efforts.

Friendly and kind, these dogs get along with all the family, although you should take care if you are introducing this lively Gundog into a household with small children.

Afghan Hound

Elegant and independent

Size 63–74 cm (25–29 in)
Weight 23–27 kg (50–60 lb)
Exercise needs 🐾 🐾 🐾 🐾
Family pet? 🐾 🐾 🐾 🐾
Maintenance 🐾 🐾 🐾 🐾

Bred for: Chasing large animals
An Afghan Hound is sensitive, energetic and free-spirited

The Afghan Hound's glamorous coat makes this one of the most elegant of dogs. It also makes them one of the most demanding to groom. When they shed their puppy coats you'll find hair everywhere, and adult dogs need brushing or combing at least once a day to remove knots, which develop rapidly.

Afghan Hounds have an aristocratic air. They are generally dignified and aloof, although some dogs have a rather clownish side. Sweet tempered and loyal, they require a patient owner who will treat them gently.

Their owner must also be prepared to give them plenty of exercise. Quiet in the home, they come alive in the open air, and will gallop and jump given space. They were bred for chasing.

They are usually sociable with other dogs but may chase small pets. Although loyal, they tend to remain a little detached, so an Afghan is not a good choice for someone who wants an intense bond with their dog.

Basset Hound

Gentle but stubborn

Size 33–38 cm (13–15 in)
Weight 18–27 kg (40–60 lb)
Exercise needs 🐾 🐾 🐾
Family pet? 🐾 🐾 🐾 🐾
Maintenance 🐾 🐾

Bred for: Hunting rabbits and hares
A Basset Hound is calm, headstrong and solemn

Easy does it: that could be the mission statement for Basset Hounds. One of the calmest and most mild-mannered of dogs, they do best in an easy-going environment. However, although they are content to doze around the house, they must have regular, steady exercise or they quickly develop weight and health problems.

Perhaps the most surprising characteristic of these dogs is the sheer volume of their bark, which they will sometimes demonstrate while walking or if they sense danger. Even when they are in the deepest of sleeps they are vocal, their big chests helping to produce quite a howl.

The drooping eyelids that are typical of the breed are attractive but make them susceptible to eye infections. Their exaggeratedly long ears are also prone to collecting dirt and, therefore, infections. It is also worth noting that their impressive jowls cause them to drool saliva.

Although slightly stubborn, the affectionate, placid Basset Hound has a generally wonderful nature and gets along with humans of all ages.

Beagle

Alert and curious

Size 33–40 cm (13–16 in)
Weight 8–14 kg (18–30 lb)
Exercise needs 🐾 🐾 🐾 🐾 🐾
Family pet? 🐾 🐾 🐾
Maintenance 🐾 🐾 🐾

Bred for: Hunting rabbits and hares
A Beagle is brave, inquisitive and energetic

One of the most independently minded of dog breeds, Beagles are rarely winners in obedience trials. However, their even temper and friendly disposition make it easy to understand why they are so popular as pets.

Energetic animals, Beagles are a dog of choice for people who relish regular, energetic exercise. However, their independent streak and a natural urge to follow a scent, means that they can be difficult dogs to walk, and they are often seen disobeying their owner's once they are off the lead. They are also easily bored.

Their short coats mean that Beagles can shake themselves dry after even the wettest of walks, and they are easy to clean after a wet and muddy outing. As befits a breed that was bred to hunt, they are particularly happy when part of a gang.

Intelligent and keen to please, they easily adapt to changes in their environment and lifestyle, but they are one of the harder dogs to train, needing firm and consistent commands. However, if you have the time and the patience, you will be rewarded with an amiable and tidy companion.

Bloodhound

Inquisitive and likeable

Size 58–59 cm (23–27 in)
Weight 35–50 kg (100–110 lb)
Exercise needs 🐾 🐾
Family pet? 🐾 🐾 🐾 🐾
Maintenance 🐾 🐾

Bred for: Tracking
A Bloodhound is strong, gentle and bright

Tough and strong-willed, Bloodhounds are nonetheless gentle and placid. However, they are most certainly not the lazy, rather dopey dogs often portrayed in popular culture. True, their exercise requirements are moderate, but they are active and playful dogs.

Bloodhounds get along well with children, but because they are large and sometimes slightly clumsy, they should be supervised if they are around toddlers. For the same reason they thrive in large, spacious homes. Once on the trail of a scent, they will pursue it tenaciously, so make sure that your garden is secure. They have a stubborn streak, which means that confidence in the owner is essential.

Although their coats are easy to maintain in good condition, Bloodhounds drool a great deal and need regular cleaning. Their ears also tend to droop into their food as they eat and have to be regularly cleaned and wiped.

These dogs' size cannot be overstated, and the broad sweep of their tail only adds to the range of destruction they can wreak. However, they are as friendly, intelligent and noble a dog as anyone could wish.

Otterhound

Cheery and friendly

Size 61–69 cm (24–27 in)
Weight 30–55 kg (65–120 lb)
Exercise needs 🐾 🐾 🐾 🐾
Family pet? 🐾 🐾 🐾 🐾
Maintenance 🐾 🐾 🐾

Bred for: Hunting otters
An Otterhound is affectionate, amiable and happy

Large, friendly dogs, Otterhounds nonetheless have strongly independent characters because they were not traditionally kept as pets, and obedience training will be a lengthy process. Happily, these cheerful and loveable dogs make up for this by being good-natured at all times.

Otterhounds adore plenty of exercise, with long runs and good swims among their favourite activities, and once they are on the trail of a scent, it is hard to capture their attention. These dogs could never be accused of being over-fastidious in keeping tidy, so owners of Otterhounds must be able to cope with their dogs' messy ways with good humour and patience. They plod around the home, rarely lifting their paws far off the floor. Easy-going dogs, they get along with everyone, although small children and pets might be accidentally knocked over.

Their powerful cry carries far and wide and might not be appreciated as much by your neighbours as it is by you. However, these are essentially even-tempered dogs that present few problems to owners with sufficient energy and a roomy enough home.

Borzoi

Amenable and faithful

Size 68–74 cm (27–29 in)
Weight 35–48 kg (75–105 lb)
Exercise needs 🐾 🐾
Family pet? 🐾 🐾 🐾
Maintenance 🐾 🐾 🐾

Bred for: Coursing wolves in Russia
A Borzoi is calm, graceful and lively

If this breed ever comes across as a little haughty, it is worth recalling that they were originally popular among the Russian nobility and aristocracy. They have distinctive noses and jaws and are magnificently impressive-looking dogs.

Although Borzois can be aloof with strangers, they are sweet, intelligent dogs that are affectionate to their owners. Generally docile, they should present few problems during training and are pleasantly tranquil and quiet while indoors.

Preferring brief, speedy exercise sessions, these dogs are ideal for agile owners who are not seeking a companion for lengthy, meandering adventures. At full speed they are a wonder to behold, but bear in mind that they are stubborn once on the chase.

The silky coat adds to their handsome appearance, but it will need regular and thorough grooming. Borzois are not given to displays of affection, but they are nonetheless devoted to their owners and will tolerate children and other pets.

Elkhound

Playful and extrovert

Size 49–52 cm (19–21 in)
Weight 20–23 kg (44–50 lb)
Exercise needs 🐾 🐾 🐾 🐾 🐾
Family pet? 🐾 🐾 🐾
Maintenance 🐾 🐾 🐾

Bred for: Hunting bears and wolves
An Elkhound is strong, vocal and curious

If you believe that dogs should be seen and not heard, then Elkhounds are not for you. However, if you – and your neighbours – are not put off by the prospect of a vocal dog, the breed has much to recommend it.

These are outgoing and independent dogs, and the fact that they were originally bred for hunting shows itself in their energetic and courageous nature. Active and nimble, they require plenty of exercise. Indeed, if they are not kept active, they will not only be unhappy but will quickly put on weight. They have a definite love of adventure, especially in colder weather.

The coarse coat is fairly easy to care for and will protect the dog adequately during the winter. However, in summer or in a warm house the dog will suffer, and hair will be shed around your home all year round.

Elkhounds are as solid in character as they are in build. With a life expectancy of up to 15 years, they are excellent family dogs. They are good with children and will protect everyone who is part of their 'pack'.

Deerhound

Calm and athletic

Size 71–76 cm (28–30 in)
Weight 36.5–45.5 kg (80–100 lb)
Exercise needs 🐾 🐾
Family pet? 🐾 🐾 🐾
Maintenance 🐾 🐾 🐾

Bred for: Hunting deer in woodland
A Deerhound is gentle, relaxed and energetic

In their approach to activity Deerhounds are paradoxical dogs. They enjoy a good run but have only moderate exercise needs. They are large and athletic, yet are quite calm and, despite their size, keep a low profile within the home. They offer, one could say, the best of both worlds.

Dignified and even-tempered are the attributes that Deerhounds evoke in most observers. They are sensitive and independent, but their inherent desire to please means they are rarely unruly or rebellious. Reserved but friendly to strangers, they are good with children although they can be dangerous with small pets.

Although regular grooming is important, the shaggy coats are fairly easy to keep clean. Despite their athleticism, these dogs are not demanding when it comes to food. They generally adapt well to changes in their surroundings or mood, perhaps thanks to their inquiring minds.

Their long, elegant heads make these companionable dogs all the more distinctive, and a home with gentle people would be ideal for one of these unusual dogs.

Irish Wolfhound

Large but gentle

Size 71–80 cm (28–31 in)
Weight 41–55 kg (90–120 lb)
Exercise needs 🐾 🐾 🐾
Family pet? 🐾 🐾 🐾
Maintenance 🐾 🐾 🐾

Bred for: Hunting in packs
An Irish Wolfhound is fast, independent and calm

No one should consider taking on the colossus that is the Irish Wolfhound as a pet without carefully thinking through what the dog's size entails. Have you enough room in your home and car for such a dog? Would you be able to lift an ill or injured dog? Do you have access to open spaces outdoors?

Given their enormous size and rapid growth, the rate with which an owner feeds and exercises a young Irish Wolfhound is vital. Too much or too little of either will quickly lead to health problems.

Despite their size, these are gentle, placid dogs, which are quite happy to laze around in the home between walks. Once they have achieved their full size, they are awe-inspiring dogs to behold, particularly on a country walk. They enjoy brisk, fast runs and can reach impressive speeds.

Irish Wolfhounds are reasonably adept watchdogs, and their huge size and authoritative air increase the general air of protectiveness they exude. Sweet and gentle, Irish Wolfhounds are impressive in every way.

Greyhound

Speedy and elegant

Size 69–76 cm (27–30 in)
Weight 27–32 kg (60–70 lb)
Exercise needs 🐾 🐾 🐾
Family pet? 🐾 🐾 🐾
Maintenance 🐾 🐾

Bred for: Coursing hares; originally from Egypt
A Greyhound is athletic, calm and composed

In the appropriate circumstances a Greyhound running at breakneck pace is an exhilarating and graceful sight. However, their speed and their preying instincts mean that their much-needed regular exercise must be given in safe, open areas.

For all the energy they exhibit while they are outdoors, Greyhounds are serene and easy-going at home. They enjoy being part of a family, and they get along well with other dogs, particularly of the same breed. Cats, rabbits and other small pets fare less well alongside this predatory breed,

however, and combining Greyhounds with such animals should be avoided.

The short, sleek coat requires little grooming. Indeed, if a dog is bathed too regularly the coat will lose its natural weather resistance. As their slender build suggests, their appetites are modest, although they are deceptively heavy to carry.

The fastest dogs in the world, Greyhounds are intelligent and sensitive. If you live near suitable areas for walking and have bundles of energy yourself, the breed could be an ideal one for you.

Lurcher

Level-headed and stylish

Size 51–61 cm (20–24 in)
Weight 12.5–14.5 kg (27½–32 lb)
Exercise needs 🐾 🐾 🐾
Family pet? 🐾 🐾 🐾
Maintenance 🐾 🐾

Bred for: Hare coursing
A Lurcher is athletic, sleek and friendly

Imagine a dog with the mind of a Collie and the explosive speed and lung capacity of a Greyhound, and you have a Lurcher. These dogs have a lifespan of about 14 years, and they will be friendly and obedient companions throughout their lives.

Lurchers do change mood when they leave home. Indoors, they are soft and gentle dogs, but once they are outdoors on a walk they become energetic and predatory. They must, therefore, only be walked off lead in safely enclosed areas so that their determined hunting instincts cannot get the better of them.

The coat is not demanding to groom, though a regular brush or comb is advisable, and they shed their coat fairly regularly. Given their intelligence and friendly natures, they are easy to train and will quickly become popular members of the family.

Always at their happiest with gentle owners who enjoy being outdoors, Lurchers are fun-loving elegant dogs who bring nothing but joy to suitably agile owners.

Whippet
Affectionate and timid

Size 44–51 cm (17½–20 in)
Weight 12.5–13.5 kg (27–30 lb)
Exercise needs 🐾 🐾 🐾
Family pet? 🐾 🐾 🐾 🐾
Maintenance 🐾 🐾

Bred for: Chasing and killing rabbits
A Whippet is gentle, kindly and independent

A contradiction lies at the heart of the Whippet: friendly and docile towards their owners, they are nevertheless robust, determined hunters. This combination of placidity and energy makes them suitable for families with children, as long as the children are adept dog handlers.

Whippets are superb sprinters, capable of reaching speeds of up to 65 kph (40 mph) over a short distance. Hunters by nature, they are also prone to chase and kill small animals, and this, coupled with their lack of traffic sense, means that controlling them on walks can be a demanding experience.

However, they have an even disposition and are friendly yet independent. They are easy to train, as long as their owners make allowance for the fact that they are easily bored. Often shy and sensitive, Whippets do not respond well to rough handling.

The fine coat requires little grooming but means that the dogs need to be protected from the cold. Fond of people and other dogs alike, Whippets are high-spirited pets.

Dachshund

Energetic and independent

Long Haired, Smooth Haired and Wire Haired

Size 20–25 cm (8–10 in)
Weight 6.5–11.5 kg (15–25 lb)
Exercise needs 🐾 🐾
Family pet? 🐾 🐾 🐾 🐾
Maintenance 🐾 🐾 🐾

Miniature Long Haired, Miniature Smooth Haired and Miniature Wire Haired

Size 13–16 cm (5–6 in)
Weight 4–5 kg (9–10 lb)
Exercise needs 🐾 🐾
Family pet? 🐾 🐾 🐾 🐾
Maintenance 🐾 🐾 🐾

Bred for: Digging out rabbits, badgers and foxes
A Dachshund is outgoing, brave and gentle

Dachshunds are appealing dogs: they are faithful, friendly and charming. Their small size makes them simple to exercise, and they are also fairly easy to groom and maintain. There are six forms of the breed, all of which are popular.

The Long Haired Dachshunds are the most gentle and docile of the bunch, and are also enormously dignified dogs. Smooth Haired Dachshunds are neat and trim, and they have an energetic, somewhat intransigent nature. Wire Haired Dachshunds are more clownish, mischievous and curious.

For each of these three forms, there is a miniature version, which shares the larger equivalent's characteristics but in a smaller body. No matter what hair type or size they are, Dachshunds have a character that is far larger than their body.

All are alert to any visitors or strangers approaching their home. They are often loud barkers, and the smaller sizes in particular have been known to emit particularly shrill outbursts. Although Dachshunds have an independent streak in their make-up, they are wonderful companions.

Wire Haired
Dachshund

Smooth Haired
Dachshund

Long Haired
Dachshund

Australian Cattle Dog

Strong-willed and powerful

Size 43–51 cm (17–20 in)
Weight 16–20 kg (35–45 lb)
Exercise needs 🐾 🐾 🐾 🐾 🐾
Family pet? 🐾 🐾 🐾
Maintenance 🐾 🐾 🐾 🐾

Bred for: Herding cattle
An Australian Cattle Dog is tough, determined and formidable

Resilient and sturdy, Australian Cattle Dogs are what one would expect of a dog that was bred to herd cattle and they should not be denied plenty of exercise and room because they have the power to protest strongly. However, when they are treated correctly they are among the most loyal of all dogs.

How did this breed encourage cattle to move? They did it by nipping at the cows' heels – in their native Australia these dogs are known as Blue Heelers – and they sometimes carry this habit with them into domesticity. This is a trait that should be discouraged as soon as it is noticed, as should their tendency to bark excessively with their loud, high-pitched voices. When it comes to training, these are dogs for owners who enjoy a challenge.

Indeed, more than with most dogs, it's important that owners make an effort to stay one step ahead of their Australian Cattle Dogs throughout the dogs' lives. Unfortunately, many people, particularly novices with dogs, are simply not equal to the challenge.

These are, however, easy dogs to groom, and their intelligence at play makes them among the most consistently interesting of dogs. In the right hands and given plenty of jobs and tasks to perform, they're fantastic and long-lived friends.

Australian Shepherd Dog

Responsive and robust

Size 46–58 cm (18–23 in)
Weight 16–32 kg (35–70 lb)
Exercise needs 🐾 🐾 🐾 🐾 🐾
Family pet? 🐾 🐾 🐾
Maintenance 🐾 🐾

Bred for: Herding sheep
An Australian Shepherd Dog is faithful, obedient and lively

Some dogs need plenty of physical exercise, and some dogs need huge amounts of mental exertion. Australian Shepherd Dogs demand lots of both. They have strong herding instincts and are extremely sharp and agile. They are also, however, very biddable and loyal to their owners.

These dogs have performed well in obedience trials, and they also excel in agility contests. Full of courage, they are protective and make effective watchdogs – few people would fancy a scrap with one – but their propensity for guarding can sometimes spill over into aggression towards strangers or chasing small pets.

Although they are easily trained, they need strong-willed and confident owners, who will set them tasks and rewards. It is vital that they know who their master is.

Territorial and robust, the Australian Shepherd is a low-maintenance breed as far as grooming is concerned, but the dogs' need for exercise and other stimulations are rarely rivalled in the dog world. They are popular among joggers and other people who enjoy strenuous exercise.

Belgian Shepherd Dog
Bright and biddable

Size 55–66 cm (22–26 in)
Weight 27.5–28.5 kg (61–63 lb)
Exercise needs 🐾 🐾 🐾 🐾
Family pet? 🐾 🐾 🐾
Maintenance 🐾 🐾 🐾

Bred for: Herding livestock
A Belgian Shepherd Dog is observant, wary, resourceful and obedient

Belgian Shepherd Dogs are active and intelligent, and given these characteristics they get along best with people who are willing to offer them plenty of physical and mental stimulation.

There are four different forms, with distinctive coats. Malinois, the only smooth-coated dogs in the breed, may be red, fawn or grey with a black overlay. Groenendael have black, long-haired coats, and sometimes white or grey hairs around the mouth. Laekenois have distinctive, wiry coats, which set them aside from the other three forms. Tervuerens have a feathery coat.

All these dogs can be wary, and they can switch from being full of life to fearful surprisingly quickly. Like many dogs with this nature, they form very close bonds with their owners, and they are generally fine with children and other pets, although their tendency to chase should be watched when they are with smaller animals.

All four types are the same basic shape and have the same characteristics, most notably agility and awareness, which are testament to their past history as livestock herders and guards. They make good watchdogs and companions.

Tervuerens

Laekenois

Groenendael

Malinois

German Shepherd Dog
Amenable and reliable

Size 58–63 cm (23–25 in)
Weight 34–43 kg (75–95 lb)
Exercise needs 🐾 🐾 🐾 🐾
Family pet? 🐾 🐾 🐾 🐾
Maintenance 🐾 🐾 🐾 🐾

Bred for: Herding sheep
A German Shepherd Dog is faithful, bright and bold

Often known as Alsatians, German Shepherd Dogs are loyal and confident. Exceptionally intelligent animals, they have been trained for use by the police and also employed as guide and guard dogs with enormous success. They are also highly popular pets around the world.

The breed's resemblance to the wolf and concern about 'dangerous dogs' has given these dogs an unjust reputation as aggressive creatures. In truth, German Shepherd Dogs are sensitive and even-tempered. They have, of course, been known to show aggression towards other pets and strangers, but they are in general far sweeter tempered than some might believe.

This is a breed that is best kept in the hands of an energetic and experienced dog handler because they are demanding in terms of both exercise and grooming. They enjoy running and playing, and with the correct guidance and training they are great family dogs, where close bonds develop.

One of the most trainable of breeds, the German Shepherd Dog is authoritative and steady. Their popularity is steady too among families who want a bold but sensitive companion in the household.

Old English Sheepdog
Fluffy and fun

Size 56–61 cm (22–24 in)
Weight 29.5–30.5 kg (65–67 lb)
Exercise needs 🐾 🐾 🐾
Family pet? 🐾 🐾 🐾 🐾
Maintenance 🐾 🐾 🐾 🐾

Bred for: Herding sheep
An Old English Sheepdog is brave, loyal and friendly

From hardworking sheepdogs to domestic pets, show dogs and television stars, the story of the Old English Sheepdog has been an eventful one, and along the way these appealing and humorous dogs have become enormously popular.

These are outgoing and happy dogs, which adore being part of a family and will join in with most activities with fervour. Fond owners will overlook the fact that this enthusiasm means they will splash in puddles, roll in mud and generally make a mess of themselves. Their fluffy coats require prolonged attention on an almost daily basis.

Generally level-headed, obedient and well-behaved with strangers, children and other pets, these dogs do on occasion explode aggressively. They are good watchdogs, with a distinctive cry.

Rustic and romping, impish Old English Sheepdogs are animals that will steal their owner's heart. They are at their happiest in a country setting, or its nearest equivalent, and with an energetic but patient owner.

Shetland Sheepdog
Amenable and sensitive

Size 36–37 cm (14–14½ in)
Weight 6–7 kg (14–16 lb)
Exercise needs 🐾 🐾 🐾
Family pet? 🐾 🐾 🐾 🐾
Maintenance 🐾 🐾 🐾 🐾

Bred for: Herding sheep
A Shetland Sheepdog is reserved, agile and vocal

When a Shetland Sheepdog tilts its head as it looks at its owner – as these dogs are wont to do – it look likes an inquisitive, outgoing dog. This is in stark contrast to their attitude to strangers and other dogs, with whom they are normally reserved.

One of the prettiest of working dogs, Shetland Sheepdogs have frilly coats with feathered legs, and magnificent almond-shaped eyes. Naturally, the coat will require continual attention to prevent tangles and to keep it in top condition.

Alert, gentle and intelligent, these are easy dogs to train, and they will be a friend to family members. Watch out, though, for their occasional tendency to nip at ankles. However, they will happily curl up with you in the evening.

These are vocal dogs, which are given to persistent barking, particularly when they're lonely, and they should not be left alone for long periods. They need only moderate exercise, however, so they are suitable for anyone with a sedentary lifestyle.

Bearded Collie

Frisky and responsive

Size 51–56 cm (20–22 in)
Weight 18–27 kg (40–60 lb)
Exercise needs 🐾 🐾 🐾 🐾
Family pet? 🐾 🐾 🐾 🐾
Maintenance 🐾 🐾 🐾 🐾

Bred for: Herding sheep
A Bearded Collie is bubbly, friendly and playful

They bounce, they chase, and they play: Bearded Collies are as charmingly effervescent as dogs can be. Combined with their delightful sense of fun is a devoted and loving nature that – together with their appealing eyes – makes them irresistible.

The sweet and happy Bearded Collie will form a strong bond with its owner and will bring joy wherever it goes. However, brimming with confidence as they are, these dog can turn rowdy and stubborn on occasion. In the right hands, however, this should be no more than a minor issue.

Truly shaggy dogs, their coats will need continual attention with a brush and the occasional bath to prevent tangles and to keep them clean. They will also benefit from regular clipping. Given their herding background, Bearded Collies have been known to carry that instinct into the home by chasing small pets and children.

It's been quite a journey for Bearded Collies, from herding sheep on farms to popular domestic companion, but their many admirers across the globe will feel it was an absolutely worthwhile voyage.

Border Collie

Task-hungry and biddable

Size 46–54 cm (18–21 in)
Weight 14–22 kg (30–49 lb)
Exercise needs 🐾 🐾 🐾 🐾 🐾
Family pet? 🐾 🐾 🐾
Maintenance 🐾 🐾 🐾 🐾

Bred for: Herding sheep
A Border Collie is energetic, responsive and bright

Border Collies seem to have retained every drop of the working tendencies they were originally bred to exhibit. As such, they need regular jobs and tasks, or they will quickly become bored and destructive.

With high levels of mental and physical energy, these dogs are delightful companions in active, lively families with at least a medium-sized home. Their stamina is immense, so their walks must be long and lively. Their coats attract dirt during exercise and will need to be brushed at least twice a week to prevent matting.

Intelligent and keen, they will respond well to training as long as it is not harshly administered. Although they tend to be naturally obedient, it is fair to say that they are not the most tolerant dogs when they are confronted by irritating strangers, and they have been known to inflict a nip on people who tease or annoy them.

They are, however, devoted to their master and will join in with any fun task you offer them. More a dog for a grown-up household rather than one containing small children, Border Collies live life with enthusiasm.

Rough Collie and Smooth Collie

Affectionate yet aloof

Size 51–61 cm (20–24 in)
Weight 18–30 kg (40–66 lb)
Exercise needs 🐾 🐾
Family pet? 🐾 🐾 🐾 🐾
Maintenance 🐾 🐾 🐾 🐾

Bred for: Herding sheep
A Collie is popular, gentle and tender

The Rough Collie is a widely recognized breed thanks to its depiction in the enormously successful Lassie movies and television series. With their graceful heads, long noses and dark brown eyes, and their magnificent long coats, these are very pretty dogs to look at.

However, these are dogs that were bred to work, and they are more than just a pretty face. They are sensitive and aloof, but behind these traits is an affectionate and biddable dog that is easy to train and will become a happy member of a home with ample room.

The Smooth Collie is similar to the Rough Collie in all major respects, apart, of course, from the coat, which is short and flat. Both dogs' coats need regular brushing, but the Rough Collie needs more grooming than the Smooth form. In summer, Rough Collies must be kept cool to avoid overheating.

Both dogs are generally well-behaved with strangers, although there have been occasions when they have been difficult with visitors. However, these gentle dogs are usually great members of any household and will enjoy participating in family ball games.

Rough Collie

Smooth
Collie

Finnish Lapphund

Statuesque and serious

Size 41–52 cm (16–20½ in)
Weight 20–21 kg (44–47 lb)
Exercise needs 🐾 🐾 🐾
Family pet? 🐾 🐾 🐾 🐾
Maintenance 🐾 🐾 🐾

Bred for: Herding reindeer
A Finnish Lapphund is playful, solid and sensible

Finnish Lapphunds were bred to live in cold climates, so their enthusiasm for summer is limited, to say the least. Neither would you be a huge fan of hot weather if you had a coarse outer coat and a thick undercoat. The males shed their coat once a year; females twice yearly.

Given their high levels of energy and intelligence, these dogs are easily bored. They need regular exercise and plentiful mental stimulation. Alert and agile, they particularly enjoy jumping to catch a ball.

Loyal and affectionate, Finnish Lapphunds get along with all members of the family, making ideal and friendly family pets. The same is true of the single-coloured Swedish Lapphund, which differs mainly from its Finnish counterpart in its vocal and curious nature, having originally been trained to bark constantly when herding.

These are sensible, sturdy and sober dogs, and their impressive stature and suspicion of strangers add to their inherent suitability as watchdogs.

Hungarian Puli

Lively and responsive

Size 37–44 cm (14½–17½ in)
Weight 10–15 kg (22–33 lb)
Exercise needs 🐾 🐾 🐾 🐾
Family pet? 🐾 🐾 🐾 🐾
Maintenance 🐾 🐾 🐾 🐾 🐾

Bred for: Herding sheep
A Hungarian Puli is bouncy, wary and obedient

Once seen, the long, corded woolly coat of a Hungarian Puli is never forgotten. In motion, the swinging cords have been compared to both a rug and to a curtain, but however you choose to describe it, the unusual coat requires a great deal of attention to keep it in good condition.

The cords must be separated frequently to avoid dirt accumulating in them. Bathing a Hungarian Puli is a considerable undertaking, and drying one is a mammoth task, taking up to 24 hours. It is, of course, possible to brush out or clip the cords, but that would be to lose one of this dog's charms.

One of its many charms, of course. Bouncy mops of fun, these are energetic, athletic acrobats, which love to run and play. They are also extraordinarily alert, and their excellent eyesight and hearing make them effective watchdogs. Enthusiastic barkers, they are heard even when they're not seen.

Popular with all ages, Hungarian Pulis make excellent playmates for children but will need to be protected from young children who may be tempted to pull at their cords. These happy dogs are, however, generally fond of people and respond well to commands.

Lancashire Heeler

Nimble and nippy

Size 26–30 cm (10–12 in)
Weight 3–6 kg (6–12 lb)
Exercise needs 🐾 🐾 🐾 🐾
Family pet? 🐾 🐾 🐾
Maintenance 🐾 🐾

Bred for: Herding cattle and catching vermin
A Lancashire Heeler is busy, playful and energetic

Lancashire Heelers were bred to herd cattle, and very good they were at it, but this does mean that in domestic surroundings they sometimes have a tendency to nip at and attempt to round up human beings and other pets. Early training can address this.

These are alert and playful dogs. If they can be included in family activities their naturally happy demeanour reaches its peak of joyfulness. They enjoy a good chase and will be busy and contented in the home as well as in the park.

The black and tan coats are easy to maintain and will respond well to occasional and brisk grooming, which will give the coats a gloss and shine that only adds to their inherent radiance. For such small dogs they have substantial appetites.

Another way in which Lancashire Heelers defy their diminutive build is with their voices: they have a stentorian bark, which they are not scared to unleash. Brave and friendly, they are enriching members of an active household.

Welsh Corgi

Alert and bold

Size 25–30 cm (10–12 in)
Weight 9–12 kg (20–26 lb)
Exercise needs 🐾 🐾 🐾
Family pet? 🐾 🐾 🐾
Maintenance 🐾 🐾 🐾

Bred for: Driving cattle
A Welsh Corgi is self-assured, determined and steady

Convivial, fox-like animals, Welsh Corgis have become enormously popular due in part to their unofficial endorsement by Queen Elizabeth II. However, it is their dependability and loving natures that make them such successful family pets.

These dogs are easy to look after thanks to their simple waterproof coats and good behaviour. There are two types; the larger Cardigan Welsh Corgi, which is also the more relaxed of the two and the Pembroke Welsh Corgi, which is somewhat more stubborn and impetuous, but both are brave and outgoing, enjoying constant activity.

Despite their small bodies, Welsh Corgis need a lot of exercise, and they enjoy combinations of brisk walks and games. For such small dogs, they are hardy, but owners need to guard against their tendency to overeat which can lead to joint problems.

These dogs are always alert and will bark if they believe their home is under threat. However, their good-mannered nature at other times makes them a loveable breed.

Pembroke Welsh Corgi

Cardigan Welsh Corgi

Staffordshire Bull Terrier

Feisty and tenacious

Size 36–41 cm (14–16 in)
Weight 11–17 kg (24–38 lb)
Exercise needs 🐾 🐾 🐾 🐾
Family pet? 🐾 🐾
Maintenance 🐾 🐾

Bred for: Dog-fighting
A Staffordshire Bull Terrier is bold, determined and muscular

These big-headed and brave dogs are typically docile and friendly towards strangers, but if they believe that their owner or home is under attack, they will defend them to the death if necessary. Welcome to the world of the Staffordshire Bull Terrier.

These feisty dogs are impulsive by nature and enjoy regular exercise. They can walk for many miles if necessary and also have the athleticism to scale fences. However, their aggression towards other animals means that they should be kept on a leash when they are in public spaces, and they should not be introduced to households where there are cats and other pets.

It's important that their owners establish their leadership early on in the relationship, and training must be carried out thoroughly to reign in the dog's excesses. On the plus side, they are simple dogs to groom.

American Staffordshire Terriers are taller and heavier than their English equivalent, and they have a friendlier nature. They also have erect ears. However, both dogs share an aggressive streak and a powerful bite. They should not be taken on lightly.

Bull Terrier
Hardy and strong

Size 53–56 cm (21–22 in)
Weight 24–28 kg (52–62 lb)
Exercise needs 🐾 🐾 🐾
Family pet? 🐾 🐾
Maintenance 🐾 🐾

Bred for: Dog-fighting
A Bull Terrier is feisty, loving, tough and stubborn

A Bull Terrier manically spinning round and round as it chases its own tail may be amusing but could signal a problem, as could some of their other energetic excesses. A Bull Terrier that feels neglected can attack furniture and wreak havoc in the garden.

However, as long as they are in suitably experienced and active hands, Bull Terriers are loving dogs and exuberant in all the best ways. They will leap onto their owner's lap to welcome them home and lick their face. They also have a great comical side, being fun and playful, and appreciate plenty of physical and mental stimulation.

Unsurprisingly, given their dog-fighting history, Bull Terriers can be difficult with other small pets. In addition to bullying other animals from time to time, they are also sometimes possessive of their food.

The Miniature Bull Terrier shares the core characteristics of the larger dog, including that formidable pain threshold and often unforgettable bite. Neither are dogs to take on lightly as an owner.

Border Terrier

Energetic and joyful

Size 25–28 cm (10–11 in)
Weight 5–7 kg (11½–15½ lb)
Exercise needs 🐾 🐾 🐾
Family pet? 🐾 🐾 🐾 🐾
Maintenance 🐾 🐾 🐾

Bred for: Hunting and killing rats
A Border Terrier is level-headed, loyal and affectionate

Judged only by appearance, Border Terriers might be regarded as rather aggressive and snappy dogs. However, although they are undoubtedly active and tough when they are exercising in the open air, they are altogether sweeter in the home.

With charming, otter-like heads and coarse coats, these dogs also have long legs, which allow them to run at great speed. They have an independent side and an easily roused liking for a hunt, and they respond best to raucous play. They are generally friendly to strangers and other dogs.

Unsurprisingly, however, given that they were bred to hunt and kill rats, Border Terriers do not always mix well with other small pets, such as cats and rabbits, and clearly a Border Terrier should never share a home with a pet rodent.

Their dense coats need to be brushed every week and will also require hand-stripping twice a year to remove dead hair. However, they are not big eaters and are fairly easy to carry and transport. Down-to-earth and good-natured, Border Terriers are agreeable household dogs.

Airedale Terrier

Confident and tenacious

Size 56–61 cm (22–24 in)
Weight 20–23 kg (44–50 lb)
Exercise needs 🐾 🐾 🐾 🐾
Family pet? 🐾 🐾 🐾
Maintenance 🐾 🐾 🐾 🐾

Bred for: Hunting and killing badgers and otters
An Airedale Terrier is feisty, determined and outgoing

A real handful of a dog, the Airedale Terrier is one of the largest of the Terriers. As long as they are in the hands of experienced and dominant owners from the dogs' early days, they go on to be outgoing, but in a good way. However, if they are not made aware early on who is the leader of the household, these dogs can become very problematic.

They are energetic, confident and muscular dogs, and they can wreak havoc in the house and also in the garden, where their mole-hunting nature can quickly devastate your lawn and flowerbeds.

Their wiry, distinctive coats will need a thorough comb at least twice a week, with a cut and shaping around eight times a year. Neither task is particularly easy because of the hardiness and crispness of the hair. These dogs are very energetic and need regular, high-octane exercise.

Airedale Terriers are natural guard dogs because they have a perfect mix of alertness, intelligence and courage. They are also fast. The challenges of owning one of these attractive dogs are part of their charm, in the eyes of their admirers.

Wire Fox Terrier

Daring and extrovert

Size 38.5–39.5 cm (14–15 in)
Weight 7–8 kg (15–18 lb)
Exercise needs 🐾 🐾 🐾 🐾
Family pet? 🐾 🐾 🐾
Maintenance 🐾 🐾 🐾 🐾

Bred for: Hunting foxes, rabbits and rats
A Wire Fox Terrier is cheeky, enthusiastic and curious

Although the Wire Fox Terrier gets its name from its coat, it could also be said that the name is a reflection of its personality. These dogs are livewires, full of zip and noise. They have truly playful natures, but be aware that they are easily aroused and have quite a tough bite.

Exercise is important for these dogs, but they are curious and spontaneous, so their owners must keep a good eye on them in the park. They love chasing balls and exploring, but they are feisty and sometimes aggressive with other animals, including cats

and unfamiliar dogs. Their lust for food reflects their energetic ways.

The only major difference between the Wire Fox Terrier and the Smooth Fox Terrier is the coat. The dense, wiry coat of the Wire Fox Terrier needs regular stripping to remove dead hair, while the Smooth Fox Terrier has dense but straight hair.

Both dogs are funny and loving with their owners. Towards strangers, however, they can be suspicious, and they must be trained and kept with a confident hand. An owner with such a hand will enjoy this breed.

Irish Terrier

Quick and keen

Size 46–48 cm (18–19 in)
Weight 11–12 kg (25–27 lb)
Exercise needs 🐾 🐾 🐾 🐾
Family pet? 🐾 🐾
Maintenance 🐾 🐾

Bred for: Hunting and killing small animals
An Irish Terrier is feisty, reactive and good-natured

Many Terriers are courageous, but Irish Terriers verge on the reckless at times. They are handsome, graceful dogs, but they are also adventurous, audacious and heedless, and they need a firm and experienced hand. They also need plenty of exercise.

Irish Terriers are often aggressive towards other dogs and smaller pets, including cats, and although their hot tempers rarely extend into their dealings with humans, their territorial nature means that even the politest of this breed are good watchdogs.

The coats do not require excessive grooming, although twice-weekly combing is necessary, as is regular hand-clipping.

Irish Terriers must be socialized and obedience-trained early in life and, given their wilful streak, this can be challenging. However, when they are in the home the dogs are calmer and better behaved than their outdoor antics would suggest. Intelligent and graceful, they know how to conduct themselves in the home, and they have a remarkable sense of humour.

Jack Russell Terrier
Excitable and charismatic

Size 23–26 cm (9–12 in)
Weight 4–7 kg (9–15 lb)
Exercise needs 🐾 🐾 🐾 🐾
Family pet? 🐾 🐾 🐾
Maintenance 🐾 🐾

Bred for: Hunting and killing rodents
A Jack Russell Terrier is feisty, determined and independent

There is a fine line between exuberance and over-exuberance – just ask the owner of a Jack Russell Terrier. These enthusiastic dogs are at their best when they're lively and excitable, just as long as they do not stray into snappy territory, where their harsh bite can inflict a nasty wound.

Experienced owners will manage to keep the worst excesses of this breed's feisty nature under wraps. A dominant stance and plenty of exercise are among the keys to accomplishing this, for these are playful dogs and should be given ample opportunities to explore and chase.

Enthusiastic and charismatic, the Jack Russell Terrier is a loving and spirited breed.

Completely unfazed by their small bodies, these dogs believe they are much bigger.

The smooth-haired and rough-haired forms both have user-friendly coats, which need only weekly brushing, although the rough-haired version will need occasional hand-stripping.

Parson Russell Terriers are lively and outgoing dogs, with a slightly mettlesome side. A high-profile breed thanks to numerous media portrayals, they have grown in popularity in recent years and make a good pet for an active family. Intelligent little scamps, these dogs are cheerful and fun, and, because they are always alert, they make great watchdogs.

Parson Russell Terrier

Jack Russell Terrier

Norwich Terrier

Cheeky yet obedient

Size 24–25 cm (9–10 in)
Weight 5–5.5 kg (11–12 lb)
Exercise needs 🐾 🐾 🐾
Family pet? 🐾 🐾 🐾 🐾
Maintenance 🐾 🐾 🐾

Bred for: Hunting and killing rodents
A Norwich Terrier is vigilant, bold, gregarious and big-hearted

A dog with wonderful contradictions in its personality, the Norwich Terrier is at once a cheeky livewire and a friendly and acquiescent friend. Low, compact and strong, these dogs do not allow their small bodies to stop them believing they are big dogs.

Insistent that they are the centre of attention, there are few occasions when Norwich Terriers are not either up to something or looking for something to get up to. They are almost busybody-like in their approach to life: intelligent and inquisitive.

The Norfolk Terrier is a close relation, and the two breeds are largely the same. Norwich Terriers have pricked-up ears, whereas the ears of Norfolk Terriers are folded down, which gives them a more gentle look.

Both breeds can be possessive of food, and they love to dig and bark. Their exuberance, if indulged, is normally a joy, which is why the most successful owners of these breeds are those who have the time and inclination to play along.

Norwich
Terrier

Norfolk
Terrier

Cesky Terrier

Sensitive and well-mannered

Size 28–35.5 cm (11–14 in)
Weight 7–8 kg (15½–17½ lb)
Exercise needs 🐾 🐾 🐾
Family pet? 🐾 🐾 🐾
Maintenance 🐾 🐾 🐾 🐾

Bred for: Killing rats and foxes
A Cesky Terrier is formidable, curious and friendly

Perhaps the most tender-natured of the Terrier group, Cesky Terriers are not overly demanding dogs. They need only moderate exercise, and as long as they receive sufficient attention, they will blend into most homes and neighbourhoods.

They can, however, be dangerous around unfamiliar small pets, particularly cats, and it is vital that they are properly socialized to avoid them becoming aggressive towards strangers. Their intake of food must also be monitored, but this is easier said than done as they are adept at sneaking snacks that were not intended for them.

Inquisitive, eager to please and sociable, these are not the kind of dog you can ignore or leave alone for long periods, and they do tend to be destructive when they are bored.

With their distinctive beards and eyebrows, these are elegant dogs, but they need regular grooming, both combing and frequent trimming, to keep their attractive coats in good shape. The results make the effort worthwhile.

Scottish Terrier
Dignified but dashing

Size 25–28 cm (10–11 in)
Weight 8.5–10.5 kg (19–23 lb)
Exercise needs 🐾 🐾 🐾
Family pet? 🐾 🐾 🐾
Maintenance 🐾 🐾

Bred for: Hunting and killing small mammals
A Scottish Terrier is scrappy, sensible and brave

It would be a foolish creature that believed that a Scottish Terrier's small stature and general air of gentleness meant they were worth picking a fight with. Once roused, this breed is bold and scrappy – with quite a bite.

As puppies, Scottish Terriers are fun-loving, sweet creatures. However, they mature into far more serious and dignified dogs, complete with a highly independent nature. To make this leap smoothly, they need early socialization. Patience and consistency are key to successful training, as these dogs can be stubborn.

Compact and sturdily built, Scottish Terriers do not require huge amounts of exercise, but given their jaunty natures they will always be receptive to imaginative activity, including ball games. Their wiry coats need brushing twice a week and clipping every six months, traditionally around the head, ears, back and tail.

Although they possess an impressive bark, Scottish Terriers will not use it without good reason. This, coupled with their staunch loyalty and territorial tendencies, makes them good watchdogs.

West Highland White Terrier
Independent and playful

Size 25–28 cm (10–11 in)
Weight 7–10 kg (15–22 lb)
Exercise needs 🐾 🐾 🐾 🐾
Family pet? 🐾 🐾 🐾 🐾
Maintenance 🐾 🐾 🐾 🐾

Bred for: Hunting and killing rats
A West Highland White Terrier is self-confident, brave and affectionate

Sometimes known simply as Westies, these are excitable and determined dogs. Add to this their stubborn and independent characters, and you have a formidable breed on your hands. But a wonderful one.

These are quintessential members of the Terrier group. Self-assured, sturdy and feisty, you will know when one is around. However, they are also cheerful and curious animals, which will join in with fun family activities, enhancing them as they do so.

Their thick coats are sometimes closer to cream than white in colour, but whatever the shade they require regular clipping and attention. Although Westies are independent dogs, they respond well to training, and they also need at least an hour of exercise each day, when they particularly enjoy activities that have a sense of adventure and purpose.

Small but strong, these dogs have a muscular build beneath their coats. Any small animals that get in their way, either inside or outside the home, risk being chased and killed. To their owners, though, West Highland Terriers could scarcely be a more loving family member.

Skye Terrier
Dignified and beautiful

Size 25–26 cm (9–10 in)
Weight 8.5–10.5 kg (19–23 lb)
Exercise needs 🐾 🐾 🐾
Family pet? 🐾 🐾 🐾
Maintenance 🐾 🐾 🐾 🐾

Bred for: Hunting and killing foxes and badgers
A Skye Terrier is wary of strangers, brave and self-assured

Were you to conclude from their elegant coats that Skye Terriers are soft dogs, you might be in for a rude awakening. They are fearless, tough and confident. They are also easily roused and have a bite that you would not forget in a hurry.

These dogs are territorial and distrustful of strangers. To their owners, though, they are loyal, loving and affectionate. They love to chase during walks and have extremely sharp reflexes. In the home they are relaxed, but they cannot be trusted around other small pets, such as cats, rabbits and rodents. Their relationship with other dogs is mixed.

The long, flowing coat conceals their large bones and sturdy build. To keep the coat in tiptop condition, daily grooming and regular trimming are essential. The tangles that form if the coat is neglected quickly wreak havoc.

Of all the Terriers, the Skye is one of the more introspective and independent. However, they form close bonds with owners and are sometimes one-person dogs. Many people find these sweet-looking dogs irresistible.

Chihuahua

Spirited and frolicsome

Size 15–23 cm (6–8 in)
Weight 1–3 kg (2–6 lb)
Exercise needs 🐾 🐾
Family pet? 🐾 🐾 🐾
Maintenance 🐾 🐾

Bred for: Companionship
A Chihuahua is playful, cheeky and friendly

You know that the Chihuahua is a small dog, but a Chihuahua would disagree with you there. They believe they are big dogs, and they are partly correct: their bodies might be small but their charm is enormous.

There are two forms of the breed – the Smooth Coated and Longhaired – but their different coats aside, all Chihuahuas share the same key traits, which normally include cheekiness, high spirits and playfulness. However, this is a breed with wide variations within it, and you are as likely to find a friendly, outgoing Chihuahua as you are to come across an introverted, suspicious one.

They will nearly always get along well with other pets, and despite a sharp bite, their diminutive build makes them relatively unthreatening. The same cannot be said in reverse though. Boisterous children can harm these dogs, as can adults who do not always watch where they step.

Neither form needs excessive grooming, although Longhaired Chihuahuas inevitably need more regular attention than Smooth Coated dogs. They are enthusiastic about exercise, but much of this can be done indoors, and these are excellent dogs for small households.

Smooth
Coated
Chihuahua

Longhaired
Chihuahua

Affenpinscher

Mischievous and independent

Size 24–28 cm (9½–11 in)
Weight 3–4 kg (6½–9 lb)
Exercise needs 🐾 🐾 🐾
Family pet? 🐾 🐾
Maintenance 🐾 🐾

Bred for: Catching rodents
An Affenpinscher is impish, sassy and headstrong

Affenpinschers are sometimes referred to as monkey terriers, and it's easy to see how they got their nickname. Cheeky, playful and busy, they have even been known to try to climb trees. Were a competition to be held to find the most clownish of dogs, the Affenpinschers would almost certainly be in the final line-up.

If any dog were to represent a bridge between the Toy and Terrier categories it is the Affenpinscher. They are very Terrier-like in character with a pronounced sense of humour and they get along best with humans who do too.

The harsh, rather rough coats do need fairly regular combing and shaping, but because the dogs look good with a slightly unruly effect, grooming need not be a time-consuming affair. Despite their outgoing natures, these dogs do not require excessive exercise and respond well to firm and consistent training.

Normally good with other dogs and small pets, Affenpinschers are nonetheless suspicious of strangers and make good watchdogs. Look out for their tendency to sulk or throw tantrums, tendencies that are easily worsened by any hint of spoiling.

Australian Silky Terrier

Responsive and friendly

Size 22–23 cm (8–9 in)
Weight 4–5 kg (8–10 lb)
Exercise needs 🐾 🐾 🐾
Family pet? 🐾 🐾 🐾
Maintenance 🐾 🐾 🐾

Bred for: Killing rodents and keeping watch
An Australian Silky Terrier is playful, brave and vocal

Although this breed is in the Toy category and has the word 'silky' in its name, this does not mean it is in any way a feeble breed. Quite the contrary, this is a noisy, brave and energetic dog.

The breed's coat needs regular brushing so that it does not become tangled or matted. They do not have an undercoat, and, like many of their human equivalents from Australia, these dogs do not like cold weather. Therefore they will need to live in a warm, comfortable home.

Australian Silky Terriers thrive on human contact and will quickly become unhappy if they are left alone for long periods. They are territorial dogs and can be aggressive towards other pets, including small dogs and cats. Raising them alongside another pet will help improve relationships.

Although they enjoy moderate exercise out of doors, Australian Silky Terriers will also find things to expend energy on in the home, and the most successful owners will relish the chance to join in with the fun.

Yorkshire Terrier

Brave and lively

Size 22.5–23.5 cm (9 in)
Weight 2.5–3.5 kg (5–7 lb)
Exercise needs 🐾 🐾 🐾 🐾
Family pet? 🐾 🐾 🐾 🐾
Maintenance 🐾 🐾 🐾 🐾

Bred for: Killing rodents
A Yorkshire Terrier is feisty, affectionate and stubborn

Are you willing to give plentiful attention to your pet? Are you happy to have a dog sitting on your lap for long periods? Then a Yorkshire Terrier could be worth considering.

Although they are tiny, Yorkshire Terriers are full of character. Their hunter heritage is seen in their gutsy, active behaviour. They will happily play with dogs much larger than them, and they can be dangerous around other small pets, such as cats. They can also be prodigious barkers.

A perfectly groomed Yorkshire Terrier is among the most attractive and distinctive of dogs, but it takes regular work to keep their coats clean and free of knots. The hair above the eyes will need trimming or tying up.

These are sharp-witted, alert dogs. They have excellent hearing, which makes them good guard dogs, and they are energetic in the home and outside, so will need regular exercise. Tough but playful, they are the ultimate lap dog.

Bolognese
Docile and devoted

Size 25.5–30.5 cm (10–12 in)
Weight 3–4 kg (5–9 lb)
Exercise needs 🐾 🐾
Family pet? 🐾 🐾 🐾 🐾
Maintenance 🐾 🐾 🐾 🐾

Bred for: Companionship
A Bolognese is tender, relaxed and loyal

Although their appearance might suggest that they are playful and rather happy-go-lucky dogs, Bologneses are among the most serious and intelligent of breeds. These are deep thinkers, and they have a special knack for solving problems and reading the body language of humans.

Don't be mistaken into thinking that these gentle, small and compact dogs are averse to a bit of play. Indeed, they can sometimes be quite rowdy while they are enjoying themselves and roaming off the lead, but their need for exercise is not excessive. The soft, flocked white coat requires regular and thorough grooming.

Their devotion to their owners can become fairly intense, and their need for company – be it from humans or other pets – is strong, and they can be rebellious and noisy if left alone for a long time. They're quick to learn and to respond to training.

The dogs' natural facial expression is exuberant and attentive, and rightly so, for these bright and interactive dogs have bags of both of these qualities. This is a fine dog for the novice owner.

Bichon Frise

Jolly and friendly

Size 23–28 cm (9–11 in)
Weight 3–6 kg (7–12 lb)
Exercise needs 🐾 🐾
Family pet? 🐾 🐾 🐾 🐾
Maintenance 🐾 🐾 🐾 🐾 🐾

Bred for: Companionship
A Bichon Frise is confident, engaging and striking

In common with many dogs with similarly extravagant-looking coats, Bichon Frises require extensive and regular grooming. Their dazzling, silky white coats, one of the key characteristics of this breed, must be brushed every day, so the breed should be considered only by people who have time to revel in the grooming ritual.

These are among the most self-assured of dogs, and they will befriend almost every human they meet – particularly those who are willing to play with them. Their playful and lively character does not mean that they are hyperactive, however. Indeed, Bichon Frises do not expect lengthy walks and are very adaptable.

With a lifespan of about 14 years, this breed has the potential to become a very good family pet. However, first-time owners in particular should be aware that these dogs are difficult to housetrain, with the females being especially tricky. Patience and persistence are important at this stage but will be thoroughly rewarded when the dog matures into an entertaining, happy and loving pet.

Havanese

Sensitive and responsive

Size 23–28 cm (9–11 in)
Weight 3–6 kg (7–13 lb)
Exercise needs 🐾 🐾 🐾
Family pet? 🐾 🐾 🐾 🐾
Maintenance 🐾 🐾 🐾 🐾

Bred for: Companionship
A Havanese is devoted, warm-hearted and fun

There is a touch of the theatrics to the Havanese breed. These bright, springy and bouncy dogs love attention and are willing to turn on the clownishness or become show-offs in order to get it.

An ideal day in the life of these dogs will also include plenty of exercise and play, and they will normally spend some time perched in a position where they can look out of a window and herald the arrival of visitors, which will be done with typical panache.

The thick double coat attracts mud and dirt during outdoor activities and must be brushed daily, so that mats and tangles do not form. Housetraining can be a problem with some members of the breed.

These dogs do have a sensitive side, and they are attentive and responsive to their owners, enjoying the company of children, making them ideal as family pets. If the whole world's a stage, the Havanese is a leading member of the cast.

Cavalier King Charles Spaniel
Regal and reliable

Size 31–33 cm (12–13 in)
Weight 5–8 kg (12–18 lb)
Exercise needs 🐾 🐾 🐾
Family pet? 🐾 🐾 🐾 🐾
Maintenance 🐾 🐾 🐾

Bred for: Companionship
A Cavalier King Charles Spaniel is frolicsome, sweet and friendly

These playful dogs are friendly and fun. Generous in their love for the young, the old and all in between, they also get along well with other family pets. It's not surprising that they have grown considerably in popularity over the last decade.

However, the growing popularity of the breed has led to an increase in instances of fatal heart conditions and other inherited health problems, so make sure that you check the full medical history of the dog before you purchase.

These dogs need reasonably regular grooming, particularly around the ears and along the feathered tail, where the hair will quickly get tangled if it's not brushed and combed. Although they require regular exercise, Cavalier King Charles Spaniels are content to adapt to the circumstances in which they find themselves.

The same is true of the King Charles Spaniel, which is smaller and somewhat less friendly. Their doleful eyes and wonderful floppy ears make both these breeds irresistibly cute, and if you are looking for an affectionate companion for all the family, a Cavalier King Charles Spaniel will be a shrewd choice.

Cavalier
King Charles
Spaniel

King Charles
Spaniel

English Toy Terrier
Determined and devoted

Size 25–30 cm (10–12 in)
Weight 2.7–3.6 kg (6–8 lb)
Exercise needs 🐾 🐾 🐾
Family pet? 🐾 🐾 🐾 🐾
Maintenance 🐾 🐾

Bred for: Hunting and killing rats and companionship
An English Toy Terrier is frolicsome, fun and vocal

The erect ears of the English Toy Terrier have been compared to candle flames, and the way these ears stand to attention mirrors the alertness of the breed. These are lively and playful dogs, which need plenty of stimulation, both physical and mental.

This is a dog that requires only minimal grooming, the short, dense coat needing little more than a quick wipe with a cloth to maintain its pleasing, glossy state. To complement the coat, the dog has dark, sparkling eyes, and these, together with the long neck, give the dog a somewhat excitable air.

English Toy Terriers are very affectionate and devoted to their owners, although they are more stand-offish with strangers. They get along fairly well with children and other pets, though young English Toy Terriers need protection from boisterous, noisy children.

Their independent character makes these dogs a challenge to train. However, in the correct hands they will mature into delightful, if somewhat noisy, companions.

Italian Greyhound
Small and speedy

Size 32–38 cm (12½–15 in)
Weight 3.5–4.5 kg (8–10 lb)
Exercise needs 🐾 🐾 🐾
Family pet? 🐾 🐾 🐾 🐾
Maintenance 🐾 🐾

Bred for: Companionship
An Italian Greyhound is sweet, quiet, needy and discerning

A dog of contrasts, the Italian Greyhound can transform itself in an instance from a laid-back dog, curled up on a blanket, into a lightning fast creature. Once they have achieved full pace, they are nimble and graceful – a wonderful sight.

These affectionate dogs are generous with their love and expect their owners to be the same. Indeed, it is fair to say that Italian Greyhounds demand attention and physical affection. For such sleek dogs they are surprisingly cuddly.

They have short, glossy coats, which require little grooming. A simple daily wipe with a chamois will keep the coats clean and shiny. Regular teeth brushing is especially important, because this breed is particularly susceptible to a build-up of plaque.

Italian Greyhounds do not need as much exercise as their larger relatives, and a daily walk with short bursts of running will keep them happy. Their short coats mean that they dislike cold weather, but their character is delightfully warm.

Papillon
Obedient and energetic

Size 20–28 cm (8–11 in)
Weight 4–4.5 kg (9–10 lb)
Exercise needs 🐾 🐾 🐾
Family pet? 🐾 🐾 🐾
Maintenance 🐾 🐾 🐾 🐾

Bred for: Companionship
A Papillon is vivacious, active, loving and eager to please

These small but elegant dogs are named for the French word for butterfly, thanks to their large, spectacular ears, and just like their insect namesakes, they are graceful, attractive and highly prized creatures.

The ears are always erect, and this gives these dogs an alert appearance, which is not deceptive, because although these are sweet-natured dogs they are also full of life and always at the ready. They absolutely adore attention and play.

As with many stunning-looking animals, Papillons place heavy demands on their owners when it comes to grooming. They should ideally be groomed daily, and they also need regular cleaning. However, their exercise needs are not excessive, and they are easily trained.

Happy and fun-loving, Papillons spread those feelings wherever they go and whoever they meet. They can be noisy animals, but they are obedient and friendly, and make excellent watchdogs. As long as you can match their love of company and energy, you should find them a successful addition to your household.

Pomeranian
Vivacious and vocal

Size 22–28 cm (8½–11 in)
Weight 1.8–2.5 kg (4–5½ lb)
Exercise needs 🐾 🐾 🐾
Family pet? 🐾 🐾 🐾 🐾
Maintenance 🐾 🐾 🐾 🐾

Bred for: Companionship
A Pomeranian is friendly, devoted and busy

Pomeranians could never be accused of lacking confidence, and although their pride can sometimes spill over into cockiness, these extrovert dogs are so delightfully affectionate that it would take a cold heart not to forgive their strutting ways.

Always ready for an adventure or a game, these dogs are forever busy and aware of everything going on around them. They have low exercise needs, and a short walk, combined with some indoor play, will normally suffice. When you take your Pomeranian out for a walk every passer-by will be noticed and scrutinized, as the dog positively dances his way down the street.

Pomeranians have a tendency to be extravagant barkers, and this must be controlled from the start so that it does not become a problem. Their harsh coats need regular attention so that tangles do not form.

With their sweet temper and bouncy temperament, Pomeranians live life to the full. Resembling miniature, rather cute foxes, they have heart-winning eyes and puff-ball coats, and their admirers would say that their huge self-confidence is completely justified.

Miniature Pinscher

Feisty and curious

Size 25–30 cm (10–12 in)
Weight 4–5 kg (8–10 lb)
Exercise needs 🐾 🐾 🐾
Family pet? 🐾 🐾 🐾
Maintenance 🐾 🐾

Bred for: Hunting rodents
A Miniature Pinscher is loving, affectionate and busy

When Miniature Pinschers are described as affectionate, there is nothing abstract about this choice of word. These dogs love a cuddle and will hop onto their owner's lap or chest and nestle there until they are removed.

It's not that these are sedentary dogs. Indeed, this is one of the busiest breeds in the Toy category. With their distinctive, prancing gait these sharp-eyed dogs like chasing, running and climbing, and they cannot always be expected to heed requests to return to their owner's heel. This is another Toy with Terrier traits.

Their short coats are shiny and simple to maintain, and an occasional brushing to remove dead hair is all that is required. Although wilful, these dogs are also very intelligent, and their keenness to learn makes them receptive to training.

Miniature Pinschers can be scrappy with other small animals. They are rough with small objects too, so do not expect any dog toys to last long in their paws. Given plenty of attention, room to explore and things to occupy their time, these dogs live their lives with enthusiasm and glee.

Pekingese
Self-assured and aloof

Size 15–23 cm (6–9 in)
Weight 4–5.5 kg (10–12 lb)
Exercise needs 🐾 🐾
Family pet? 🐾 🐾 🐾 🐾
Maintenance 🐾 🐾 🐾 🐾 🐾

Bred for: Companionship
A Pekingese is stubborn, vocal and sweet

These pretty but diminutive dogs have two characteristics that sometimes surprise potential owners: they are vocal and fearless. Among their many attractive qualities, therefore, is the fact that they make effective if unlikely guard dogs.

A less surprising fact about the breed is that the thick, long coat needs regular grooming to prevent mats from forming. You should be aware that the long feathery fur will also attract dirt galore on walks.

Their short legs and breathing difficulties mean that Pekingese tire easily and have low exercise requirements. Indeed, given how quickly they overheat, they should not be considered by people who want to spend long days out or summer holidays with their dog.

An independent and superior character, the Pekingese expects regular attention but can be somewhat aloof in return. They thrive in a relaxed household with older, more considerate children. They are suitable for a first-time owner, provided they have the patience and ability to maintain the beautiful, complicated coat. These dogs are also fine for those with limited space.

Pug
Solid and friendly

Size 25–28 cm (10–11 in)
Weight 6.5–8 kg (14–18 lb)
Exercise needs 🐾 🐾
Family pet? 🐾 🐾 🐾
Maintenance 🐾 🐾

Bred for: Companionship
A Pug is robust, playful and loyal

Stocky and proud, Pugs really know how to carry themselves with aplomb, and their sturdy appearance is matched by their character, which, though loyal, is also determined and firm.

They are among the most distinctive of all dog breeds, with their short, glossy coats, thick necks and tightly curled tails. Their radiant eyes are hard to resist. They are easy to keep clean and well groomed, and they are also fairly simple to train, slotting in easily to a variety of households.

Pugs appreciate regular exercise, but they tire quickly so are far from being the most demanding dogs in this regard. Do not let their stocky build lead you to think that they are slow movers, however – they can move far faster than you would imagine.

Companionable and confident, Pugs are even-tempered and physically balanced. Their natural gait is forward-leaning, and, although their expression is serious, they are fun-loving. There is almost something of the Bulldog about this Toy breed.

Bulldog

Courageous and compassionate

Size 31–36 cm (12–14 in)
Weight 23–25 kg (50–55 lb)
Exercise needs 🐾 🐾
Family pet? 🐾 🐾 🐾 🐾
Maintenance 🐾 🐾 🐾

Bred for: Bull- and bear-baiting and dog-fighting
A Bulldog is brave, friendly and determined

The phrase 'the Bulldog spirit' has become part of the lexicon of life, but the dogs are actually more docile and friendlier than their appearance and reputation might suggest. They are certainly bold, protective and stubborn, but much of the ferocity they once had has long since been bred out of them.

Although their glossy coats are generally straightforward to maintain, Bulldogs have folds of skin on their faces and around their tails, and these need regular, ideally daily, cleaning. Be aware, too, that snoring, wheezing and drooling are all common traits among Bulldogs.

Their build and the fact that their shortened muzzles restrict breathing mean that these dogs are not keen on extensive or energetic exercise. Their breathing problems are exacerbated by hot weather, and they find it hard to regulate their temperature, so cold snaps are a problem, too.

Usually tenacious, Bulldogs are a challenge to train. However, they are protective and caring towards their owners.

French Bulldog

Affectionate and lively

Size 56–61 cm (22–24 in)
Weight 23–25 kg (50–55 lb)
Exercise needs 🐾 🐾
Family pet? 🐾 🐾 🐾 🐾
Maintenance 🐾 🐾 🐾

Bred for: Companionship
A French Bulldog is endearing, playful and laid-back

Do not judge these dogs by the serious, rather glum expression they often have on their faces. They are actually wonderfully sweet and fun-loving dogs, which thrive on human attention. Indeed, some are little short of clownish.

As puppies, French Bulldogs are frisky and playful, but as they mature into adulthood they become far more relaxed, although their newly acquired placidity does not make them any less clingy. They love nothing more than a doze with their owner, so get on well with those who have sedentary lifestyles.

Their shortened noses make breathing difficult, and this can lead to their wheezing when awake and snoring while asleep. These problems are particularly pronounced during hot weather or if the dog is tense. Their coat itself needs little care, but the wrinkles on their face will require daily cleaning.

These dogs have only modest requirements for exercise, and most will be more than satisfied with a daily walk on a lead. Fun and affectionate, they love contact with their owners and with their sturdy build are better suited to older children.

Dalmatian

Elegant and gritty

Size 56–61 cm (22–24 in)
Weight 23–25 kg (50–55 lb)
Exercise needs 🐾 🐾 🐾 🐾
Family pet? 🐾 🐾 🐾 🐾
Maintenance 🐾 🐾 🐾

Bred for: Running alongside carriages
A Dalmatian is sleek, affectionate and tireless

This is one of the most distinctive and widely recognized breeds, and the dogs are extremely popular. Indeed, Dalmatians have plenty to recommend them: their dignity and athleticism are probably unrivalled in the dog world, and as a breed they could hardly be more friendly.

Dalmatians love to run, and they have high levels of energy and stamina. They will jump at the chance to join their owner on a jog, bike ride or adventurous walk, and unless you are fit and energetic yourself, a Dalmatian is probably not the dog for you.

The enchanting black or liver-coloured spotted coat is another of the breed's charms. The hair is short and requires only minimal grooming, although regular brushing is recommended to remove dead hair. These happy dogs have long tails, which will wag more or less perpetually.

Dalmatians can be aggressive towards strange dogs, but they get along well with most other animals, particularly horses. With people, Dalmatians are friendly, affectionate and outgoing. They can live to a good age and remain active runners to the end.

German Spitz

Brave and active

Klein

Size 23–29 cm (9–11½ in)
Weight 8–10 kg (18–22 lb)
Exercise needs 🐾 🐾 🐾
Family pet? 🐾 🐾 🐾
Maintenance 🐾 🐾 🐾 🐾

Mittel

Size 30–38 cm (12–15 in)
Weight 10.5–11.5 kg (23–25 lb)
Exercise needs 🐾 🐾 🐾
Family pet? 🐾 🐾 🐾
Maintenance 🐾 🐾 🐾 🐾

Bred for: Working on farms and companionship

A German Spitz is self-assured, brave and energetic

These are bold and determined little dogs. They come in two forms, the Klein and the slightly larger Mittel, but apart from the difference in size, the two dogs share the same characteristics. They respond well to commands and adore the chance to join in with family games and walks.

With their pricked-up ears and alert expression, these are dogs that enjoy stimulation. Both forms have luxurious coats that keep them warm in cold weather. However, the breed's grooming needs are not for the uncommitted, for not only does the double coat require considerable care and attention but these dogs are not always the most patient of groomees.

Although they are not large dogs, if you approach the home of a German Spitz you will prompt a chorus of noise as they alert their owner to your imminent arrival. They are also territorial dogs, and they can be troublesome with other pets in the household.

These are not an ideal choice for the first-time owner, but experienced owners will find them rewarding dogs to own. Inquisitive and bold, they are enjoyably challenging pets.

Mittel

Klein

Japanese Spitz
Autonomous and alert

Size 30–36 cm (12–14 in)
Weight 5–6 kg (11–13 lb)
Exercise needs 🐾 🐾 🐾
Family pet? 🐾 🐾 🐾 🐾
Maintenance 🐾 🐾 🐾 🐾

Bred for: Companionship
A Japanese Spitz is affectionate yet aloof with strangers

Do not let the brilliant white coat of a Japanese Spitz fool you into concluding these are high-maintenance dogs that require endless grooming. They do not. Obviously, the thick two-layered coat will need attention, but the texture of the coat means that dirt falls off it easily, and the undercoat remains dry.

Although these dogs are affectionate and loyal towards their owner, they are suspicious of strangers, which makes them good guard dogs. They are attentive and playful, and they get along well with other pets and with children, including toddlers, for whom they display adequate patience.

Watch out for a tendency to bark. If your dog exhibits this trait it must be tackled early in their life to prevent it becoming excessive. Their exercise demands are moderate, although they do enjoy being outdoors and appreciate regular walks and agility games. Their appetite for food is greater than their small stature would suggest.

Agile and courageous, these little dogs have a delightful coat and an excellent character, especially with children.

Giant Schnauzer

Affectionate and courageous

Size 60–70 cm (23½–27½ in)
Weight 32–35 kg (70–77 lb)
Exercise needs 🐾 🐾 🐾
Family pet? 🐾 🐾 🐾 🐾
Maintenance 🐾 🐾 🐾 🐾

Bred for: Herding and guarding cattle
A Giant Schnauzer is brave, dependable and indefatigable

The hair on the face of a Giant Schnauzer grows in such a way that the dogs have a beard and moustache that are both attractive and distinctive. The dogs have a sturdy, powerful appearance, which is one reason why they are popular as guard dogs.

The other reason for their popularity among those seeking guard dogs is that they have alert, intelligent and discriminating minds. Few other dogs have a greater sense of who is welcome and who is not. They can be difficult with other dogs, particularly when both dogs are male.

There are also Miniature and Standard Schnauzers, which are distinguished more by size than by temperament. However, both the smaller forms are fonder of human

company than their Giant counterpart. The Miniature dogs also have slightly less demanding coats.

Schnauzers are good at picking up the moods of the people around them, and they become strongly attached to their owners and enjoy being close to them at all times. All three forms need plenty of free-running physical exercise.

**Miniature
Schnauzer**

Giant Schnauzer

Standard
Schnauzer

Shar Pei

Strong-willed and individualistic

Size 46–51 cm (18–20 in)
Weight 16–20 kg (35–45 lb)
Exercise needs 🐾 🐾 🐾
Family pet? 🐾 🐾
Maintenance 🐾 🐾 🐾 🐾

Bred for: Dog-fighting and hunting
A Shar Pei is aloof, tranquil and brave

The distinctive folds of loose skin add to the seemingly frowning expression of the Shar Pei, but these are not unhappy dogs. However, they are sombre and semi-detached by nature, so if you are looking for a playful friend you should avoid this breed.

If, however, you like the idea of an independent dog, you could do worse than have a Shar Pei. They are easy dogs for a confident owner to train, are well-mannered in the home and require simple grooming. Calm and collected, they are happiest in homes that are correspondingly tranquil.

These dogs are not over-demanding when it comes to exercise – a brisk walk will suffice. However, those famous wrinkles can be the cause of painful health issues,

including in-rolling eyelids, and they must be cleaned with a moist cloth every day.

Although reserved, these dogs are loyal, affectionate and protective of their family.

The Shar Pei's distinctive wrinkles require daily cleaning to avoid skin sores.

Poodle

Spirited and calm

Toy Poodle
Size 25–28 cm (10–11 in)
Weight 6.5–7.5 kg (14–16½ lb)
Exercise needs 🐾 🐾 🐾
Family pet? 🐾 🐾 🐾
Maintenance 🐾 🐾 🐾 🐾

Miniature Poodle
Size 28–38 cm (11–15 in)
Weight 12–14 kg (26–30 lb)
Exercise needs 🐾 🐾 🐾
Family pet? 🐾 🐾 🐾 🐾
Maintenance 🐾 🐾 🐾 🐾

Standard Poodle
Size 37.5–38.5 cm (15 in)
Weight 20.5–32 kg (45–70 lb)
Exercise needs 🐾 🐾 🐾 🐾
Family pet? 🐾 🐾 🐾 🐾
Maintenance 🐾 🐾 🐾 🐾

Bred for: Retrieving birds from water; Miniature Poodles for companionship
A Poodle is lively, obedient and good-natured

Poodles are intelligent, active and easily trainable dogs. Their coats do not shed, so they are popular with people who suffer from allergies to dog hair. The coats do need regular clipping, however, and some owners like to clip them into extravagant designs.

There are three forms of this popular dog. The largest is the Standard Poodle, which are exceptionally smart and obedient dogs. They are more energetic than the other, smaller forms, loving nothing more than a run or a swim. They normally get along well with other pets. When you are buying a Standard Poodle make sure that you acquire a dog that comes from good stock and with no inherited diseases.

Miniature Poodles are lively and playful. They are sensitive and loyal dogs, and they

Standard
Poodle

sometimes become particularly attached to one person. With their manageable build and obedient nature, these are very popular family dogs indeed.

Despite their size, Toy Poodles are confident dogs that enjoy human interaction. However, they can be harmed by over-exuberant children. Like the Miniature, the Toy is probably better suited to town life.

They can be vocal but are dependable, and their high spirits are always good natured.

This is a breed with a number of health concerns, including a propensity for hip problems and heart defects. As with all breeds, a potential owner should take care when acquiring one of these dogs. As long as sensible caution is exercised at that point, a great friend could be added to your home.

Toy Poodle

Miniature
Poodle

Shih Tzu

Playful and affectionate

Size 25–27 cm (10–11 in)
Weight 4.5–7.5 kg (10–16 lb)
Exercise needs 🐾 🐾
Family pet? 🐾 🐾 🐾 🐾
Maintenance 🐾 🐾 🐾 🐾

Bred for: Companionship
A Shih Tzu is noble, alert and independent

Shih Tzus were once the dogs of choice of the Chinese aristocracy, and it may be this heritage that has contributed to their character, which combines a sense of nobility with a distinctly regal and somewhat superior air.

These appealing little dogs have a wide-eyed expression that would melt the hardest of hearts. Their long, dense coats are another of their visual charms, but the dog's owner will need to put in long hours of grooming to keep it pretty and clean, particularly after wet and muddy walks, and although Shih Tzus do not require much exercise, they need a lot of cleaning after most outdoor games and activities.

A perfect pet for a family, Shih Tzus adore company, affection and play. That said, they have a stubborn and independent streak, which makes their training and upkeep more challenging than their cute appearance would initially suggest.

Bouncy and outgoing, Shih Tzus are great fun and are worth considering if you have a small home. Surprisingly devoted and protective for such a small and pretty dog, they particularly reward outgoing and affectionate owners.

Tibetan Terrier

Lively and wilful

Size 36–41 cm (14–16 in)
Weight 8–14 kg (18–30 lb)
Exercise needs 🐾 🐾 🐾
Family pet? 🐾 🐾 🐾 🐾
Maintenance 🐾 🐾 🐾 🐾

Bred for: Guarding and companionship
A Tibetan Terrier is frolicsome, friendly and gentle

Highly suitable for families, Tibetan Terriers love to run, romp and play, and they will expect to be included in most group activities among those that they know. Because their feet resemble snowshoes, they even enjoy playing in snow.

All this activity means that they are high-maintenance dogs when it comes to grooming. Their long coats attract plenty of mud and dirt on walks, and the coat quickly becomes matted and tangled if it is not brushed every day. Their hair will grow over their eyes unless it is tied back or clipped short on a regular basis.

Despite their high energy levels, Tibetan Terriers are sensitive and charming. They enjoy a snooze in the house and are loyal and friendly to their owners. Although they can be aloof and distrustful with strangers, this makes them adept guard dogs.

Given the combination of activity and grooming needs, this is not a dog to be taken on lightly. However, they will bring much joy to a suitable household.

Boston Terrier

Sensible and outgoing

Size 38–43 cm (15–17 in)
Weight 6.8–11.5 kg (15–25 lb)
Exercise needs 🐾 🐾 🐾
Family pet? 🐾 🐾 🐾 🐾
Maintenance 🐾 🐾 🐾

Bred for: Companionship
A Boston Terrier is thoughtful, generous and grand

Given the large, expressive eyes and the enquiring facial expression, it's little wonder that people continue to fall for the charms of the Boston Terrier. These dogs are especially popular among the more active elderly, and they are often one-person pets.

However, the Boston Terrier is one of those breeds that shows considerable variation from dog to dog, and you might have a jovial, excitable dog or a more serious, placid one. However, they are almost invariably sensible, sensitive and thoughtful towards their owners and are, in fact, well disposed in their dealings with all humans.

Their eyes can be susceptible to injury, and the dogs can find it difficult to breathe through their short noses. Many of these dogs do not tolerate heat well. However, their coats require little attention.

The short muzzles and rather square heads give these dogs a handsome, debonair look, and as their many admirers will happily attest, they are balanced and sturdy in both physique and character.

Chow Chow

Quiet and aloof

Size 46–56 cm (18–22 in)
Weight 20–32 kg (45–70 lb)
Exercise needs 🐾 🐾
Family pet? 🐾 🐾
Maintenance 🐾 🐾 🐾 🐾

Bred for: Hunting and food
A Chow Chow is quiet, self-contained and calm

Chow Chows are one of the most reserved and self-contained of all dogs. They might physically resemble lions, but there the similarity ends for they are well-mannered, quiet animals, which are perfectly content to mind their own business.

These dogs do need regular exercise, but their stilted gait means that they do not much enjoy activities that are either strenuous or particularly playful. They are not excessively keen to please and so get along well with owners who are not seeking a dog that is in any way subordinate to them.

Their plush coats need brushing once or twice a week, and this can be a time-consuming task. The thick coat makes the dogs uncomfortable in particularly hot or humid weather. In general, these dogs are not keen on being handled, particularly by strangers, and in the wrong hands on a hot day, they can be temperamental.

Chow Chows have distinctive dark blue-black tongues and mouths.

Leonberger

Statuesque and enthusiastic

Size 65–80 cm (25½–31½ in)
Weight 34–50 kg (75–110 lb)
Exercise needs 🐾 🐾 🐾
Family pet? 🐾 🐾 🐾
Maintenance 🐾 🐾 🐾

Bred for: Resemblance to a lion on a German coat-of-arms

A Leonberger is confident, frolicsome and energetic

One of the oldest of the German breeds, Leonbergers are large, noble and elegant dogs. When they are puppies they enjoy a range of activities, from running to pulling sleds and swimming, but as they mature their energy levels decline noticeably and they require less exercise.

With their powerful and resonant bark and assured stance, these dogs would seem to be good guard dogs. However, they are actually gentle and not at all aggressive, so their role is more that of a deterrent than a physical guard. They are generally good with other dogs, pets and people.

The coat needs brushing every day, and the dog's ears and teeth need particular attention. They have huge paws which will bring plenty of mess into the home after a walk, and they have a tendency to drool. They are big eaters, too.

These are physically affectionate dogs, and they do not cope well with long periods of isolation. They like to jump up onto their owner and are also renowned for leaning against their owner's legs to express their devotion. Ideally, they need an experienced owner who will feel comfortable with their boisterous expressions of love.

Mastiff

Territorial and courageous

Size 70–76 cm (27½–30 in)
Weight 79–86 kg (175–190 lb)
Exercise needs 🐾 🐾
Family pet? 🐾 🐾 🐾
Maintenance 🐾 🐾

Bred for: Guarding
A Mastiff is brave, protective and formidable

The broad chest, heavy body and mouth full of huge teeth give the muscular Mastiff a formidable appearance. They are also among the most courageous of dogs. However, appearances can be deceptive, for this is one of the most gentle and docile of breeds.

Brimful of intelligence, Mastiffs adore and crave human contact, and they are loving and protective towards their owners. These enormous dogs need large, spacious accommodation because they will be unhappy and unwittingly destructive in cramped surroundings. They are extremely capable watchdogs and will keep all but the most foolhardy of would-be intruders from their home.

Mastiffs enjoy exercise, but, perhaps surprisingly for such large dogs, they do not require a great deal of it. Regular walks will keep them happy, but they cannot be expected to accompany joggers. Although their coats require no special attention, their propensity to drool, caused by their loose jowls, creates its own problems.

These affectionate and considerate dogs are loyal, but not in an overly showy manner. This reserved nature also makes them calm members of the household.

Bullmastiff

Loyal and rumbustious

Size 61–69 cm (24–27 in)
Weight 41–59 kg (90–130 lb)
Exercise needs 🐾 🐾
Family pet? 🐾 🐾
Maintenance 🐾 🐾 🐾

Bred for: Guarding
A Bullmastiff is brave, constant and strong

Generally a docile dog, the Bullmastiff is, if roused, a formidable prospect, and this decidedly wilful breed's first requirement is a confident, patient owner, who is strong in both body and mind.

Given such an owner, these lively dogs have much to recommend them. They love bonding with their owner and are as good-natured as dogs come. Moreover, the combination of keen alertness, fierce loyalty and fearlessness makes them exceptionally effective guard dogs.

They do not require excessive exercise, but to avoid weight problems in later life these somewhat lazy dogs will need to be chivvied along. These are dogs that love their homes, and they will not appreciate being left outdoors. They are not keen on hot or humid weather.

Bullmastiffs are quick to learn and will respond well to an owner who is good-natured but provides firm leadership. Once the correct relationship has been established, owner and dog will have great fun together.

Bernese Mountain Dog
Solicitous and affable

Size 61–69 cm (24–27 in)
Weight 40–44 kg (87–90 lb)
Exercise needs 🐾 🐾 🐾
Family pet? 🐾 🐾 🐾
Maintenance 🐾 🐾 🐾 🐾

Bred for: Pulling carts
A Bernese Mountain Dog is self-assured and affectionate

People who like the idea of a friendly giant in their household often choose a Bernese Mountain Dog. Tall, powerfully built and active, these are nonetheless among the most good-natured and even-tempered of breeds.

Well-mannered companions, they are brimming with an endearing blend of courtesy and courage. They appreciate a spacious home and are keen on company. They get on well with most children, although they should not be left alone with toddlers because of their large, heavy build and enthusiastic nature.

The long, wavy tri-coloured coat is another of the breed's charms. It will need daily brushing and regular washing, and these dogs tend to shed hair heavily during the summer season. Among other health problems these dogs are susceptible to are elbow and hip conditions, and they tend to dribble saliva uncontrollably.

Rarely noisy, almost always friendly and intelligent, the Bernese Mountain Dog makes a fantastic, protective companion and a good family pet, particularly for people who live in the countryside.

St Bernard

Steadfast and dependable

Size 61–71 cm (24–28 in)
Weight 50–91 kg (110–200 lb)
Exercise needs 🐾 🐾
Family pet? 🐾 🐾 🐾
Maintenance 🐾 🐾

Bred for: Pulling carts
A St Bernard is generous, strong and protective

St Bernards are handsome dogs, and they are particularly captivating as puppies. Before falling for their charms, however, it is vital that you think about just how big and strong they eventually become. This doesn't just mean that they need plenty of room, it also signifies a ravenous appetite, which makes them expensive animals to keep.

The breed's many admirers will not let any of this deter them, of course, and they point to the breed's ardent and loyal nature. St Bernards have low exercise demands, are friendly with children and pets and have a laid-back, sensible disposition.

It is the dogs' appearance that appeals to most people. Upstanding and solid, they have huge heads and feet. Their jaws, too, are substantial affairs, which add to their charm. Eager to please, St Bernards are simple to train and despite their size, they are relatively straightforward to groom.

Despite their forlorn facial expression, St Bernards are contented, mellow dogs.

Boxer

Playful and acrobatic

Size 53–63 cm (21–25 in)
Weight 25–35 kg (55–70 lb)
Exercise needs 🐾 🐾 🐾 🐾 🐾
Family pet? 🐾 🐾 🐾
Maintenance 🐾 🐾 🐾

Bred for: Capturing game
A Boxer is persevering, affectionate and lively

Boxers are distinctive dogs, not just in appearance but in character too. Lively and sociable, their sense of fun is rarely bettered in the dog world. However, they should be considered only by energetic owners, and ideally those who already have some experience with dogs.

These dogs are best suited to spacious surroundings, and although they are affectionate, they should not be introduced into a family with toddlers or young children. Their playful nature makes Boxers good companions for older children. They will also get along well with other pets.

The short, glossy coats, which may be fawn or brindle with white markings, require little grooming and attention, but the breed's short nose can make breathing difficult, and they often have problems with saliva control.

Intelligent, self-assured and alert, Boxers are inquisitive dogs. Training must be done by a dominant figure, although given their intelligence they will learn fast. They become hopelessly devoted to their owners.

Dobermann
Powerful and faithful

Size 65–69 cm (25–27 in)
Weight 33–37.5 kg (73–83 lb)
Exercise needs 🐾 🐾 🐾 🐾 🐾
Family pet? 🐾 🐾 🐾
Maintenance 🐾 🐾 🐾

Bred for: Guarding
A Dobermann is intrepid, lively and strong

There are few more loyal and courageous breeds than the Dobermann. Alert and intelligent, the dogs have much to recommend them as pets, but they are also among the more demanding of breeds.

These dogs must be firmly trained by a dominant owner, who will let them know who is the head of the household. Endlessly energetic, they demand plenty of exercise and will also expect a commensurate amount of food.

With their low-maintenance short, shiny coats and athletic yet muscular builds, they have a visual grace that belies their – somewhat exaggerated – reputation for ill-tempered aggression. Nevertheless, given their height and power, they are best suited to families with both older children and previous experience of dog ownership. They should not be introduced into a family where there are other pets.

Dobermanns expect and need plenty of attention and stimulation, and they have been known to bond particularly strongly with one family member. Devoted and protective, these dogs will repay the effort that is put into their training and upkeep by being the perfect guard dog.

Pinscher

Tenacious and obedient

Size 43–48 cm (17–19 in)
Weight 11–16 kg (23–35 lb)
Exercise needs 🐾 🐾 🐾 🐾
Family pet? 🐾 🐾 🐾
Maintenance 🐾 🐾

Bred for: Hunting and killing rodents
A Pinscher is determined, lively and responsive

Sharp, intelligent and alert, Pinschers are always on the ball, and when they fix you with that intense stare, it is hard to ignore them. However, owners must not allow this somewhat intimidating habit and self-assured temperament of theirs to confuse the hierarchy of the household.

Pinschers are full of energy and curiosity, and are very responsive and easy to train. However, they sometimes have a manipulative streak, which must not be encouraged. They are territorial dogs, and will not surrender gladly if they find themselves in a confrontational situation.

Although they normally get along well with other dogs, Pinschers should not be introduced into households with non-canine small pets – they will chase and, in all likelihood, kill cats or rabbits. However, these Working Dogs are normally fine with children.

These dogs can be possessive and vocal, but they require little special grooming and are not excessive eaters. Nimble and bright, they are rarely dull characters.

Great Dane

Convivial yet independent

Size 71–76 cm (28–30 in)
Weight 46–54 kg (100–120 lb)
Exercise needs 🐾 🐾 🐾 🐾
Family pet? 🐾 🐾 🐾
Maintenance 🐾 🐾 🐾

Bred for: Hunting game
A Great Dane is strong, confident and interactive

Highly distinctive-looking dogs, Great Danes are often viewed as the ultimate dog. Large and playful, they are dependable and friendly and brimming with intelligence. It's not surprising that they are such a perennially popular breed.

Do not let the relaxed state they adopt when they are at home fool you into believing that Great Danes do not enjoy exercise. Once out and about, they greatly appreciate long walks and make suitable jogging companions.

The breed's short, dense coat, which comes in five official colours – brindle, fawn, blue, black and harlequin – is easy to maintain, and these dogs rarely need bathing, which is a good thing given their immense size and weight.

The ideal Great Dane owner will be experienced with dogs and willing to be firm yet gentle during training. They will have a large home, with any precious ornaments stored well out of the way of this somewhat blundering breed. They will also be able to afford the enormous food bills. Although one of the more independent of dogs, Great Danes become firm friends with their owners and are good guard dogs.

Rottweiler

Protective and bold

Size 58–69 cm (23–27 in)
Weight 41–50 kg (90–110 lb)
Exercise needs 🐾 🐾 🐾 🐾 🐾
Family pet? 🐾 🐾
Maintenance 🐾 🐾 🐾

Bred for: Flushing and retrieving birds
A Rottweiler is determined, audacious and territorial

Calm, playful and affectionate. Applying these three adjectives to Rottweilers might cause a few eyebrows to rise in some quarters, but it's important to remember that this breed has had an enormously unfair press in recent times, which belies their good nature.

Rottweilers are intimidating dogs, of course, and they can exhibit aggression to both strangers and unsuitable owners. A strong character is essential during and after training. More than most breeds, they need to know who is the head of the pack.

The short black and tan coats are easy to maintain, and a little extra grooming effort to promote the natural shine will be worth it. The real demands of this breed come with exercise. Although they are relatively quiet while they are indoors, they will expect two hours or more of walks each day.

Certainly not dogs for the inexperienced owner, Rottweilers are responsive and territorial, and when they are trained and handled correctly, these intelligent characters will instil a feeling of immense pride in their successful owners.

Alaskan Malamute

Rugged and resilient

Size 58–71 cm (23–28 in)
Weight 38–56 kg (85–125 lb)
Exercise needs 🐾 🐾 🐾 🐾 🐾
Family pet? 🐾 🐾 🐾
Maintenance 🐾 🐾 🐾 🐾

Bred for: Pulling sleds
An Alaskan Malamute is distinguished, independent, heavy and loyal

If the prospect of a strong, powerful and hardy dog is attractive, you might want to consider an Alaskan Malamute.

These are enjoyable but challenging dogs to own. For a start, you will need to teach them early on that you are not a sled for them to pull down the street during walks. Walking an Alaskan Malamute is an unforgettable experience. If you are unable to meet their ferocious demands for exercise, they can become boisterous and destructive, and given their bulk, a destructive Alaskan Malamute is something to be avoided.

Despite their size, these dogs are at heart affectionate and dignified. They become fond of their owners and will be loyal to a fault. They are also wonderfully intelligent dogs, whose independent streak will be a plus for many owners.

These are formidable yet trusting dogs. Vigorous at play, the dogs appreciate company and fun on a regular basis.

Siberian Husky

Lively and extrovert

Size 51–60 cm (20–23½ in)
Weight 16–27 kg (35–60 lb)
Exercise needs 🐾 🐾 🐾 🐾 🐾
Family pet? 🐾 🐾 🐾
Maintenance 🐾 🐾 🐾 🐾

Bred for: Pulling sleds
A Siberian Husky is energetic, affectionate and keen

The perfect companions for energetic runners, Siberian Huskies are full of life. They also have a strong independent streak and are therefore among the more challenging of dogs to train and exercise.

Their sense of independence can be something of a challenge to inexperienced owners, who would be better looking elsewhere, as would any would-be owner who is short on energy. Suitable owners, however, will delight in their Siberian Huskies, relishing their keenness to please, their general affability and their honest, outgoing character.

By nature, these dogs prefer to live in packs, and in the home they need and expect regular attention. A predatory breed, they will not mix well with small dogs or other pets, and are wary of strangers and children, although they will spread their love evenly throughout a family unit.

The long coats keep them warm during the harshest of winters, of course, but they can lead to them suffering in warmer weather. They require daily grooming, and even then they will shed hair throughout the home. Jumpy yet gentle, Siberian Huskies are high-maintenance and loveable dogs.

Choosing the right dog for you

The best dogs for allergy sufferers

Bichon Frise

Chihuahua

Irish Terrier

Poodle (all forms)

The best dogs for children

Beagle

Bernese Mountain Dog

Boxer

Bulldog

Cesky Terrier

Chesapeake Bay Retriever

Golden Retriever

Labrador Retriever

Tibetan Terrier

The best dogs for a first-time owner

Affenpinscher

American Cocker Spaniel

Australian Silky Terrier

Beagle

Bernese Mountain Dog

Bolognese

Cavalier King Charles Spaniel

Cesky Terrier

Collie

Golden Retriever

Havanese

Labrador Retriever

Pekingese

Pug

Welsh Springer Spaniel

Whippet

The best dogs for high exercise

Afghan Hound
Airedale Terrier
Alaskan Malamute
Bearded Collie
Belgian Shepherd Dog
Border Collie
Boxer
Chesapeake Bay Retriever
English Springer Spaniel
Golden Retriever
Gordon Setter

Greyhound
Irish Red and White Setter
Labrador Retriever
Otterhound
Pointer
Rottweiler
Siberian Husky
Staffordshire Bull Terrier
Standard Poodle
Yorkshire Terrier

The best dogs for low exercise

Bloodhound
Chihuahua
French Bulldog
Japanese Chin
King Charles Spaniel
Papillon
Pekingese
Pug
St Bernard
Shih Tzu
Yorkshire Terrier

The best dogs for low grooming demands

Basset Hound
Beagle
Boston Terrier
Boxer
Bull Terrier
Bulldog
Foxhound
Mastiff
Pointer
Pug
Labrador Retriever
Rottweiler
Weimaraner
Welsh Corgi

The best dogs for longevity

Australian Cattle Dog
Border Terrier
Bullmastiff
Chihuahua
Dalmatian
Dobermann
Jack Russell Terrier
Miniature Dachshund
Standard Poodle
Toy Poodle

The best dogs to be a watchdog

Airedale Terrier
Australian Silky Terrier
Boston Terrier
Chihuahua
Dachshund
Pinscher
Fox Terrier
German Shepherd Dog
Miniature Poodle
Miniature Schnauzer
Rottweiler
Scottish Terrier
Shih Tzu
Standard Poodle
West Highland White Terrier
Yorkshire Terrier

Index

Acknowledgements

Executive editor Trevor Davies
Editor Ruth Wiseall
Executive art editor Mark Stevens
Designer Peter Gerrish
Production controller Carolin Stransky

Picture credits

DK Images/Tracy Morgan 49, 67, 72
John Daniels 103
Octopus Publishing Group Limited/Angus
Murray 21, 31 top, 33, 34, 35, 39, 43, 65, 83,
85 top, 87, 95, 107 top, 107, 111, 115, 117,
119 top, 119 bottom, 121; 123, 125, 127,
131, 133 top, 133, 135, 139, 141, 145, 147,
153, 155 top, 155 bottom, 158, 159 bottom,
159 top, 160, 161, 164, 165, 167, 169, 171,
177, 182, 183, 197; /Ray Moller 29 centre
right, 29 bottom right, 45, 75, 101, 109 top,
109 bottom, 113, 129, 149, 191, 193;
/Russell Sadur 61; /Steve Gorton 14, 17, 19,
23, 25, 27, 29 top left, 31 bottom, 37, 40,
41, 47, 51, 53, 55, 57, 59, 63, 65 top, 65
centre, 69, 71, 73 top, 73 bottom, 77, 79, 81,
85, 89, 90, 93 top, 93 bottom, 97, 99, 105,
137, 143, 151, 157, 163, 172, 173, 175, 179;
181, 185, 186, 189, 195.